A TIME TO DIE

NICOLAS DIAT

A Time to Die

Monks on the Threshold of Eternal Life

Translated by Mary Dudro

Illustrated by David le Merrer

IGNATIUS PRESS   SAN FRANCISCO

Original French edition:
Un temps pour mourir:
Derniers jours de la vie des moines: récit
© 2018 Librairie Arthème Fayard, Paris

Cover art:
Saint Francis with a skull in his hands
c. 1630, School of Francisco de Zurbarán
Found in the collection of the State Hermitage, St. Petersburg
Heritage Image Partnership Ltd./Alamy Stock Photo.

Cover design by John Herreid

For my friend Robert Cardinal Sarah

CONTENTS

FOREWORD

A Time to Die is the title of Nicolas Diat's new book. What audacious simplicity, but also what great faith to dare approach such a question that, conventionally, it is practically forbidden to discuss. But, as always, Nicolas Diat has written with great skill and depth. He leads us to the abbeys to help his readers enter into the mystery of death.

Monasteries are places where one learns to live and die in an atmosphere of silent prayer, the gaze always turned toward the beyond and the One who made us and whom we contemplate—because "from my flesh I shall see God" (Job 19:26). All those who pray consider life, the world, and death with confidence and emotion, and, at every moment, discern the presence of God within them. It is certain the monks, too, are familiar with the difficult and tragic reality of death. They experience the anguish, the fear at the approach of the "6:00 A.M. bus that disappears into the darkness". But, in these elevated places of prayer, since the Resurrection of Christ, death is an Easter, a passage. We lay aside the bodily exterior with which we could not move into the divine atmosphere. Those who leave us, like Brother Vincent-Marie de la Résurrection, at the abbey of Lagrasse, Father Dominique, at En-Calcat, Brother Buisson, at Solesmes, Father Joël, at Mondaye, and the magnificent hermits of the Grande Chartreuse, Dom Landuin, Brother Jean, Dom Gabriel, Dom André Poisson, continue to live, to know, to love, without being limited by the fragility of their bodies or hindered by the

9

shackles of sin. Their death is a passage into a life that man has prepared here below and that God continues without end. Death places us in the infinity and depths of God.

In reading *A Time to Die*, we better understand that death is the most important act of earthly existence. All life is made to explode, to go farther, to merge with Life, with God.

I am infinitely thankful to Nicolas Diat for having brought us for a moment before the mystery of death, and I recommend to all the reading of this wonderful book.

Robert Cardinal Sarah
Prefect of the Congregation for Divine Worship
and the Discipline of the Sacraments

EXTRAORDINARY STORIES

> Vanity of vanities, says the Preacher, vanity
> of vanities! All is vanity.... For everything
> there is a season, and a time for every matter
> under heaven: a time to be born, and a time to die;
> a time to plant, and a time to pluck up what
> is planted.... All go to one place; all are
> from the dust, and all turn to dust again.
>
> —Ecclesiastes 1:2; 3:1–2, 20

In Rome, at the foot of the Via Veneto, behind the Fountain of the Bees, the crypt of the Capuchin church presents a strange sight. From floor to ceiling, five chapels are ornamented with the bones of monks from ages past. At the entrance, a somber wooden placard warns visitors: "We were like you; you will be like us."

Embalmed monks, fixed in perpetual stillness, re-clothed in their habits, imitate postures of prayer. Fibulas, tibias, humeri, and femurs decorate the walls and arches. Piles of bones, heaps of skulls, vertebrae, and ribs that give form to the most sophisticated creations now compose a surrealist reverie.

"The greatest hoax of the Capuchins is that they impose the adoration of their dead victims upon the living." In *La Reine Albemarle ou le dernier touriste* (Queen Albemarle or the last tourist),[1] the story of a trip to Italy, Jean-Paul Sartre thus mocks the *delirium* of these religious.

---

[1] Jean-Paul Sartre, *La Reine Albemarle ou le dernier touriste* (Paris: Gaillimard, 1991).

These macabre ornaments intensify sorrowful passions. They betray a disordered relationship with death. One would like to believe that this is merely a parody or carnival pantomime. When one leaves the crypts to return to life, the din of Roman traffic reveals charms we never noticed before.

This baroque exultation is the perfect antithesis to the denial of death that pervades our present times. Modern man has an obsessive fear. He does not want to admit that life has an end. He searches by every means to forget the Grim Reaper. Death is disguised with makeup, like a hated and nightmarish reality. God is dead, and so is death. The *Homo deus* runs like a madman who seeks to catch the flag of immortality by force.

Alas, it is enough to enter a funeral home one day, where undertakers reign supreme, in order to perceive the success of this utopic vision. A new extreme was reached when a novel funeral practice arrived from the United Sates: the liquefaction of bodies through alkaline hydrolysis. The prophecy of Aldous Huxley's *Brave New World* is upon us.

In 1995, François Mitterrand wrote the remarkable preface for Marie de Hennezel's *La Mort intime* (Intimate death).[2] Tired and ill, the president of the Republic was himself at the end of life's path. "Never before, perhaps, has the relationship to death been so impoverished as in this time of spiritual desolation when men, in their rush to exist, seem to avoid all mystery", he lamented. Raised in Jarnac, he loved the countryside world where men died in their homes. Family, friends, neighbors came to keep vigil over the body of the deceased. Often, the departed

[2] Marie de Hennezel, *La Mort intime* (Paris: Robert Laffont, 1995).

reposed in the same bed where he had rested during life. The family themselves took care of the body. The shutters of the bedroom were closed. After the funeral Mass, the casket traveled through the village to the cemetery. For many months, the family would dress in black as a sign of mourning.

Since that not-so-long-ago era, the West has worked hard to bury death more deeply in the vaults of its history.

Today, the liturgy of death no longer exits. Yet fear and anxiety have never been as strong. Men no longer know how to die.

In this desolate world, I had the idea to take the path of the great monasteries in order to discover what the monks might have to teach us about death. Behind cloister walls, they pass their existence in prayer and reflection on the last things. I thought their testimonies could help people understand suffering, sickness, pain, and the final moments of life. They have known complicated deaths, quick deaths, simple deaths. They have confronted death more often, and more intimately, than most who live outside monastery walls. I had an intuition, when I began this work, that the monks would not hide anything from me, that they would tell me truthfully about the death of their members. The accounts collected in the abbeys I visited did not disappoint me.

I would like for this book to offer some hope, because the monks show us that a humane death is possible. Twenty-first-century man is not condemned to lonely endings, without love, in anonymous hospital rooms. Twenty-first-century man is not condemned to the false humanity of a death disguised and distorted in disembodied funeral parlors.

Today, the monks are perhaps the last remaining people who can understand the words of Saint Francis of Assisi's "Canticle of Brother Sun":

> Praise be to you, my Lord,
> for our sister Corporeal Death,
> from whom no living man can escape.
> Sorrowful are they who die in mortal sin;
> happy are they whom she finds living according to
>   your will,
> for the second death can do them no harm.

The saint of the Middle Ages no doubt also knew the apothegms of the Desert Fathers. In these accounts attributed to the hermits who populated Egypt during the fourth century, one can read a number of descriptions of the deaths of the first monks in Christianity. That of Abba Sisoes is especially remarkable:

> It was said of Abba Sisoes that when he was at the point of death, while the Fathers were sitting beside him, his face shone like the sun. He said to them: "Look, Abba Anthony is coming." A little later he said, "Look, the choir of prophets is coming." Again, his countenance shone with brightness and he said: "Look, the choir of apostles is coming." His countenance increased in brightness, and lo, he spoke with someone. And the old men asked him, "With whom are you speaking, Father?" He said: "Look, the angels are coming to fetch me, and I am begging them to let me do a little penance." The old men said to him, "You have no need to do penance, Father." But the old man said to them, "Truly, I do not think I have even made a beginning yet." Now they all knew that he was perfect. Once more his countenance suddenly became like the sun and they were all filled

with fear. He said to them: "Look, the Lord is coming and he's saying, 'Bring me the vessel from the desert.'" [And at that moment, he gave up his spirit.] Then there was as a flash of lightning and all the house was filled with a sweet odour.[3]

The stories told me by the Benedictines of En-Calcat, Solesmes, and Fontgombault, the Trappists of Sept-Fons, the Cistercians of Cîteaux, the Canons of Lagrasse, the Premonstratensians of Mondaye, and the hermits of the Grande Chartreuse are all as beautiful and exceptional as the memorable stories from ancient times.

The death of Abba Sisoes reminds me of the courage of Brother Vincent, a young canon crippled by multiple sclerosis, of the lucidity of Dom Landuin, a Carthusian eager to rejoin heaven, and of the grandeur of Brother Pierre, an old lay brother, pious and generous.

On the Bourbon moors, at Sept-Fons, and by the banks of the Creuse, at Fontgombault, the monks spoke to me of the radiant, peaceful, and luminous deaths of the friends of God.

These men are not heroes. Their fears, their sorrows, their torments are very real. The high walls of the monastery do not change anything about death. Sickness can become cruel, and the extremities of suffering can crush the body. What is exemplary about the monks is to be found elsewhere.

It lies in their humility and simplicity. When death approaches, and its hand reveals its strength, the monks remain the same. They are like happy and naïve children who wait with impatience to open a gift. They have no doubts about the fulfillment of the promise.

---

[3] *The Sayings of the Desert Fathers*, trans. Benedicta Ward (Trappist, Ky.: Cistercian Publications, 1975), 214–15.

In *Cinq méditations sur la mort, autrement dit sur la vie* (*Five Meditations on Death: In Other Words ... On Life*),[4] François Cheng offers us this delicate poem:

> Do not forget those in the depths of the abyss,
> Without fire, lamp, consoling cheek,
> Helping hand ... Do not forget them,
> Because they remember flashes of childhood,
> Bursts of youth—life echoing in
> Fountains, in the driving wind—where will they go
> If you forget them, you, God of memory?

In order not to be forgotten by God before leaving this world, we have much to learn from the monks. Their humanity, their courage, and their sincerity command admiration.

These keys open many doors.

---

[4] François Cheng, *Five Meditations on Death: In Other Words ... On Life*, trans. Jody Gladding (Rochester, Vt.: Inner Traditions, 2016), 94.

I

A Life Cut Short

Lagrasse Abbey

On July 19, 2014, I came for the first time to the village of Lagrasse. In the middle of the hilly and dry Corbières, the abbey of the Canons Regular of the Mother of God was still unknown to me. Despite the banks of the Orbieu, connected by the Pont-Vieux with its delicate arches, and the orderly gardens surrounding an elegant wall, the monastery seemed to me hieratic and imposing. The heavy iron gates, the main courtyard, the aristocratic façades gave the impression of entering an Occitan castle.

The buildings, which harmoniously combine Carolingian, Roman, and classical elements, the cloister of fiery, yellow sandstone, the imposing refectory, the subtle light in the abbey church, the canals of living water: history surfaces in the smallest of stones. Lagrasse is a place where the spirit breathes.

The religious looked fine in their large white habits. At the head of the community, Father Abbot Emmanuel-Marie, a rigorous and ascetic Breton, had a pleasing air about him. When he welcomed me to Lagrasse, shortly after my arrival, I knew straightaway that I had met an upright, intelligent, and humble man.

The thirty-five Augustinians who live within these walls are young. They come from all over France. Often, brilliant careers had been offered them. They preferred the service of God.

One morning, I was in the gardens and fields that surround the monastery. The wind that swept down the hills made the summer heat bearable. The canons, protected by their worn, straw hats, were busy in the huge vegetable gardens. I took a path lined with old olive trees that crossed the property. It opened onto a vast prospect of vineyards and valleys. I did not expect to find the monks' cemetery deep in the meadows.

At the entrance of the enclosure, I stopped by a freshly dug grave, poorly covered with a tarp that the wind had displaced. I remained bewildered a long while in front of this large pit. The scene left little room for doubt; the monks were preparing to bury one of their own. The rest of the cemetery, nearly abandoned, only increased my confusion. I went back forthwith, deciding to forget this macabre discovery.

On the way back, I entered the cloister. The faint trickle of a fountain enlivened the midday silence. A religious was enjoying some fresh air in the arcades. He was in a large medical chair. Beside him, seated on a small bench, an infirmarian watched his every move. Passing in front of the young canon, I was struck by the vigor of his gaze. And by his fatigue, his fragility, too. I did not dare make a connection with the walk that had led me to the cemetery.

After lunch, I asked a canon about the identity of the mysterious invalid. I remember how his words, like lightning, came crashing down: "That is Brother Vincent-Marie. He is thirty-six years old. He suffers from multiple sclerosis." Then I asked him: "This morning, I discovered a grave in the cemetery …" The answer fell, inexorable: "Yes, it is for Brother Vincent."

My anger and my sadness were silent. How could God abandon a young monk? How could he allow death to prowl around a young man at the dawn of his life?

Multiple sclerosis is a sickness that attacks the central nervous system, the brain, the optic nerves, and the spinal cord. Its symptoms vary: numbness of a limb, blurred vision, sensations of electric shock in the body. The disease progresses in stages and, after a few years, leaves permanent consequences. Movement control, sensory perception, memory, speaking become difficult, then impossible.

Brother Vincent-Marie de la Résurrection, formerly Benoît Carbonell, a canon of Lagrasse Abbey who died at thirty-eight years of age, was suffering from rapid and progressive multiple sclerosis. He was born on March 15, 1978, and he died in his monastery on Sunday morning, April 10, 2016.

A monk enters an abbey in search of God. He chooses to devote his days to prayer, to the salvation of souls. Disease and the prospect of death radically change the existence of all men. I wanted to know if it was the same for religious. Did Brother Vincent fear death? Did he feel any particular

anxiety when the passage became more evident? Did he
fight to put off the inevitable? Who was this young canon
walled up in the little room of an infirmary?

Benoît Carbonell grew up in a farming family in Normandy, where he experienced a simple and modest childhood. Joyful, cheerful, early on he showed a natural
instinct for fixing things. Without any particular taste for
studying, he chose to become an electrician. On his parents' farm, the young man had a workshop where he collected an incredible number of objects of all kinds. Later
on, he arrived at the abbey with a small truck filled with
radiators, neon lighting, electrical circuits, and light bulbs.

Brother Vincent never fully left behind his native Norman land, the hunting parties, country gatherings, or good
fellowship. He had strong sense of family and loved his
parents, his brothers, and his sister. For him, abandonment
to God was not an easy path. Brother Vincent entered
Lagrasse as a novice in 2005. He already knew he was sick.
Toward the age of twenty, he had to receive a triple vac-
cine, a common practice in his profession. Later on, the
doctors explained to him that that is when the multiple
sclerosis no doubt began.

Benoît interpreted his illness as God's way of catching
him since he had rejected his vocation. The sclerosis led
him to enter religious life. He had asked himself questions
for many years. But he always put off making the decision.
The electrician loved life, the world, and he did not see
any reason to enclose himself inside four walls. Simple,
upright, transparent, he had always had a deep faith, but
he wanted to practice his trade and stay with his friends.
One day, he confided to Father Emmanuel-Marie: "It was
thanks to the illness that I entered." The first tremors of
pain allowed him to take the big step.

When he arrived, the canons had just taken possession of the abbey walls. Lagrasse was dilapidated, the roofs were leaking, drafts of air blew everywhere. The novice was familiar with early construction sites, the heroic times when the religious restored the old monastery with their own hands. He repaired some of the electricity in a large eighteenth-century building built by the Maurists.

Brother Vincent remained marked by the lessons and good sense of his peasant childhood. One day, a mouse entered the study hall. He got up and crushed it with a simple stomp of his heel.

The year 2006 was that of his first religious vows. The illness had expanded its domain. The young man began to tremble. His right hand had been the first to go. He decided to be left-handed. Soon, both hands had failed him. From then on, he had difficulty holding his tools. For him, not being able to use a drill or screwdriver was a suffering. Without faltering, he passed on his knowledge of electricity to the brothers so they could take over and work without him.

Brother Vincent thought that the disease would last thirty years. He dreamed of a peaceful existence. The canon knew that he was vulnerable, but he was convinced that religious life would enable him to overcome his suffering.

During the course of our discussions, Father Emmanuel-Marie remembered with emotion the moment when God made use of the discovery of the illness to accelerate the decision of the young Norman: "Heaven brought down the psychological barrier of a man who had his share of weakness, egoism, and fear. Brother Vincent said himself that he had lacked generosity. The beginnings at Lagrasse were difficult. We were twenty-four brothers. The canons lived two to a room, without heating.

The brothers slept in the hallways or in storerooms, and we did the dishes in an old bathtub. The window panes were broken, the cold reigned supreme. The winter of 2005 was glacial, wet, and windy. Brother Vincent lived roughly and courageously during that pioneering period. But the destitution accelerated the progress of his disease. He thought that monastic life was going help him: it did the opposite."

Father Michel, sub-prior of Lagrasse, a brilliant and cultured religious, has always thought that the story of Brother Vincent was part of a plan willed by God. This canon from Marseille knew Brother Vincent from his arrival onward, during the time when the brothers had embarked on an ambitious project to restore the abbey. They had a sense of youth, fullness, power: "Brother Vincent entered without reserve into this adventure. He passed his days with his box of tools and his ladder. He drilled holes in all the abbey walls. At Lagrasse, they are one and a half meters thick. Our life was harsh. In the beginning, we occupied two small rooms. We had to install running water. From a human perspective, the situation might have seemed crazy. We were supported by the charity that bound us together. The canons had no idea what the weakness or sickness of a brother might be like. When the symptoms of multiple sclerosis became more evident, the disease entered for the first time into our lives. We had to purify our ambitions."

In the beginning, Brother Vincent was not accepted with perpetual vows in mind, but as a simple regular oblate. The canons did not know if he could stay, and the young Norman was well aware of the axe that threatened him. The novice changed in character. His caustic and keen humor was not the same. He who had loved to make people laugh with little strokes of irony, aware that his candor and humor were pleasing, covered himself in a respectful modesty and reserve. Doubts tormented him.

With the support of Brother Pierre, his uncle and core-ligionist at Lagrasse, he began to take serious steps with doctors to benefit from care that would improve his con-dition. Brother Vincent dreamed of being cured. He was made for happiness. He loved the joys and sorrows of community life. In a way, he was not born to be sick.

In 2008, Brother Vincent had a hard time accepting the help of a cane. His legs began to play bad tricks on him. He moved with difficulty and stumbled against the walls. The trembling of one hand, then of the entire arm, made it impossible for him to walk straight. One morning, one of his legs finally let go; he could never again walk properly.

After much equivocation, the canons decided to orga-nize his move from a room on the second floor to one on the first, in order to bring him closer to the places of community life. He was deeply upset about it. But he no longer had the strength to climb two floors.

His energy and tenacity were never lacking, as Father Emmanuel-Marie testified: "At that time, he received care at a center specializing in multiple sclerosis and muscular diseases. He was in a unit with about fifty other patients. In one week, he had visited all the patients. Brother Vin-cent had a passion for evangelization. He said rosaries, dis-tributed medals, talked about the saints. But he returned drained, exhausted, and empty. After ten days of hospi-talization, he had lost eleven pounds. Our little brother wanted to live. He was incapable of resting. During his visits to Toulouse, he did all he could to convert the med-ical teams. We found him with two or three nurses seated on the edge of his bed. They were listening to him speak about his faith. On the other hand, if he had to respond to questions in order to evaluate the progress of the disease, he lied so as not to show the extent of his suffering. Brother Vincent did not want to complain. The doctors often told him they dreamed of patients who possessed a little of his joie de vivre."

Little by little, Brother Vincent began to understand that his condition would never improve. He was thirty-five. In the prime of life, how could one accept that the end of his life was so near? Brother Vincent was no exception to this rule. He fought. For a long time the combatant had the last word.

The symptoms of sclerosis are small stones that become more and more painful. Pain infiltrates every corner. Little by little, the body resembles an old quilt that's been mended all over. Disease, disagreeable and malicious, is very theatrical. It is the knife making noise on a plate in the refectory when the hand trembles, the book that goes flying in the choir of the church, the repeated falls in the hallways. The canons became firemen who put out fires. The spiral of a cursed hourglass constantly leaped before their eyes. Each deterioration called for a solution in order to continue to believe. A missal wedged under the arm in an attempt to read and sing in the choir, prepared meals, weighted utensils, a new room; life tried desperately to regain the upper hand.

In this respect, Brother Vincent's ceremony of final vows was an intense moment that left a mark on the canons of Lagrasse. They were gathered in the Chapter room. Brother Vincent was in the middle of the room. He could not hold the candle or ritual book. At the moment when he pronounced the words that would commit his life, all his limbs trembled. Brother Vincent had the character of heroes who do not want to surrender. He loved God with all his might, but he wanted to remain on his little piece of earth.

During a walk in the hills of pines and cypresses that surround the abbey, I remember a conversation with Father Michel. I asked him if monks had a difficult time parting with earthly pleasures. His answer was simple: "Religious life does not prevent us from loving the earth. We love it differently, and perhaps more, because the earth is more beautiful with the eyes of faith. Nature is more beautiful, souls are more beautiful, human relationships are more beautiful. Brother Vincent had extraordinary adventures through his apostolates. How can one mourn such intense joys? He loved to convince men of the existence of God. He converted his nurses by helping them discover spiritual writings. Since he could no longer read, they would sit beside him daily to read him a few pages. Brother Vincent chose titles that matched their personalities to make sure they would be touched."

The mystery of Brother Vincent is the same as that of all human life. Men are drawn upward, but their bodies and their intelligence keep them on earth. Human laws are true for all, even men of God: fear of death, fear of grief, fear of forgetting are instinctive in each of us.

In 2012, the descent to the infirmary was a new trial for the brother. The canons knew he would never reenter the communal rooms. Father Michel presented to Brother Pierre plans for a new infirmary equipped especially for Brother Vincent. Brother Pierre looked at him with sadness and said: "We're not going to put him in a hole, are we?" Brother Pierre was hanging on; he did not want life as they had known it to end. In moments of doubt, the imagination easily turns toward "those mourning-chambers where old death-rales ring",[1] as Baudelaire says.

One day, in the new medical room, Brother Vincent exclaimed: "I have just asked God to be able to go quickly to heaven. But I told him to do as he pleased."

Yet, the sick man did not want to speak of death. He was not ready. On multiple occasions, when Father Emmanuel-Marie asked him if he would like to depart, he showed his desire to stay alive.

Beginning in 2013, Brother Vincent had difficulties communicating. His mind went blank at times. How can you accompany someone toward the hereafter when he can no longer speak? The brothers tried to help him construct sentences. They suggested responses. For a while, he was able to pronounce the first syllable of words. At the end, when he could no longer say anything, facial expression and touch replaced sentences.

In May 2015, his father died from a heart attack. The canons were afraid that he would die of sadness. He was so upset that he was constantly choking. The young man could have let himself die. No doubt he was hanging on so as not to leave his mother alone. The following winter was particularly violent. Nights of anguish succeeded each other without respite. Brother Vincent always put off the moment of going to the hospital. He was afraid. He knew he could die there where he did not feel as well surrounded as at the abbey. He decided to await God in his monastery.

With astounding aplomb, he lied by omission to the doctors in order to leave the hospital. Brother Vincent tried

[1] Charles Baudelaire, "Obsession", in *The Flowers of Evil*, trans. James McGowan (Oxford: Oxford University Press, 2008), 151.

hard to make them believe his condition was improving, and he achieved his goal. He left in an ambulance explaining to the medical staff that he was well. After two days, he returned.

All the canons knew the extent of his suffering. The infirmarian at Lagrasse gave the doctors a radically different description of that than Brother Vincent had. He had incredible strength of conviction and took it upon himself not to reveal anything. His smile, his joy, his peace broke down all the barriers.

At the monastery, Brother Vincent enjoyed the constant attention of the canons. When he was doing poorly, a brother slept next to his bed, on a simple mattress on the floor. Brother Vincent was reassured by this presence. The brothers came to accept being awakened multiple times in the night. And, around five forty-five in the morning, they left for the church for the office of Matins.

Over the years, the monastery acquired exceptional medical competence. But the attacks of the sclerosis became more and more barbaric. Brother Vincent struggled with mucus that choked him and could be fatal. He never agreed to a tracheotomy, refusing several times this difficult intervention that the doctors recommended. Brother Vincent was afraid of dying during the operation. He did not want to be mutilated. Sometimes, the infirmarians had literally to turn him over by holding him by the feet to help him spit. Horror moved into the room. And yet, Brother Vincent maintained this painful decision and asked pardon for all the efforts made on his behalf.

The little invalid became a puppet deprived of muscles. He was falling apart. Brother Vincent prayed he would not die during a choking fit. People affected by the same pathologies often have similar fears. What could be worse than dying by suffocation? The sick desperately search for air, their muscles contract. In those moments, Brother Vincent's facial expression could be terrible. He was relieved when the canons installed a sophisticated breathing assistance system in his room. But his terrors never disappeared. The dread of suffocation and the fear of lonely nights were twin anxieties. Brother Vincent needed the physical presence of the community. They had to find the balance between overprotection and brotherly help. Alone, the sick man did not close his eyes at night, but he was able to rest if the religious stayed near his bed. Only then, he slept like a sparrow.

In recalling Brother Vincent's suffering, Father Emmanuel-Marie was full of emotion: "He was afraid. He was afraid of dying alone while choking. Mental sufferings are as important as physical ailments. The day when he stopped speaking, how could we understand his distress, his discomfort, his pain? He often said: 'I gave everything to Jesus. He has taken everything. I thank him.' This is the fruit of a long road, a perilous route, the education of a soul. He did not surrender himself out of generosity but out of love. The acceptance of his sickness was asceticism. I told him several times that he should let go. When his father died, and he was so weak, I encouraged him: he could depart. He knew that the canons were torn. But we were ready. I sensed that he wanted to fight. Fifteen days before his death, I asked him not to stay if his reason for living was the community's pain. Brother Vincent searched me with his big eyes, then he stared into space for a long time. Finally, he blinked to signify he had understood. I did not know what he wanted, but he had heard me. I took his hand and told him the brothers would greatly mourn his death; most importantly, it was his choice, his freedom, his decision. Deep inside, I hoped God would come for him."

The brothers now had to provide delicate palliative care. Every day, they feared they would make a mistake. They knew the difference between end-of-life care and more aggressive life-prolonging treatment. In these situations, it is possible to make someone suffer by miscalculating his hydration, an excess of water causing the production of mucus. Every day, the infirmarians risked inflicting extra suffering on the sick man. His doctors questioned whether the mismanagement of the quantities of water did not lead to extra suffering.

Father Emmanuel-Marie would never forget the days when every moment was a battle: "In forcing a body to stay alive, we are not helping the soul. But I did not have to make the difficult decisions. Brother Vincent helped me. I told him he could leave to keep us from artificially keeping him in his body. 'You are no longer made to stay on this earth. We have shared extraordinary moments. You have been a Christ child, like an infant whom we had to swaddle, and a suffering Christ, in the throes of unjust suffering.'"

A monastery is not a hospital. The community had the crushing responsibility of a man who was going to die. "We made a good decision by keeping him within our walls", Brother Emmanuel-Marie confided in me. "The choice was not easy. Would we be up to the task? Could we respond to his needs? Would we be able to ease his suffering? Brother Vincent hollowed us out. The final weeks were the breaking point. The corporeal shell was used up like a fabric that no longer has any fibers. One could still wear the clothing, but it was ripping everywhere. His flesh could no longer hold his soul. It was too damaged. His death was the liberation of a soul that had become a prisoner. Facing the disease, Brother Vincent was like a little lamb led to slaughter. We tried to protect him as best we could."

In the final weeks, he no longer prayed. It would be more accurate to write that he could no longer pray. For the canons, when a man suffers martyrdom, he still prays. The suffering body itself becomes a prayer. The brothers reassured him on several occasions because he was worried about no longer knowing how to pray. He could not finish a rosary. He stammered, he stumbled, he gasped. The sick man wanted to say his prayers as if suffering had not taken hold. It was not easy to make him change his mind.

Brother Vincent wanted to live his death and go to the end of his road. He did not want anyone to steal his death from him. He was living with multiple sclerosis in a confrontational manner, and he was rousing himself to respond to the violence of the medical treatments. God had accepted that his body was crumbling, but he allowed him the freedom of his own end. Brother Vincent departed in his own way, surrounded by his loved ones, protected and cherished. The more he advanced toward God, the less his brothers understood him. Physically, the canons, the doctors, the infirmarian, were close to him; spiritually, Brother Vincent moved farther and farther away. No one could join him.

Brother Vincent had waited to die until his mother was at his side. The season was not an easy one for leaving the work of the farm. Marie-Josèphe Carbonell returned from Normandy on a Saturday. That evening, she stayed alone with her son. Saying the rosary by his bedside, she sensed that he was praying intensely.

On Sunday, April 10th, around nine o'clock in the morning, his mother came into his room. All of a sudden, the infirmarian sensed that he was about to die. The young Brother Benoît was keeping watch. He ran to find

Father Emmanuel-Marie to tell him that he must come as quickly as possible. His uncle, Brother Pierre, was in the courtyard. He was able to be present at the moment when Brother Vincent gave up his soul to God.

Brother Vincent died with great ease. Listening to Father Emmanuel-Marie, it seemed to me like hearing a man speak about the death of his own child. "I leaned over him, I knew his last moments were approaching. I told his mother to take his right hand and his sister to take his left. His body was burning hot. I recited the prayers of the dying, and I gave him the sacrament of the sick. Suddenly, we sensed that he was at peace. The little brother seemed more at rest, carried away on a journey that transcended him. We were certain that he was going to leave us. He had become transparent. The times of crises, the times of suffocations went away. He was no longer swimming in that ocean of suffering which was his prison. Brother Vincent had no fear. His departure was sweet. The day before, spasms had distorted his face. At the hour of death, he was radiant."

The last breath, the last look, the last beating of his heart had an air of victory. At the sound of the death knell, the brothers arrived. In the room where Brother Vincent had just died, they knelt down. A few moments after his death, the community was around him. They looked on the beautiful face of the one who was dead. The brothers were crying, the brothers were praying.

At the end of the morning, the infirmarians were busy with the young deceased. They asked the canons to leave the room. The time for women had come. The Father Abbot felt as if they were embalming the body of Christ before placing him in the tomb.

Brother Vincent remained six days in the mortuary chapel. A few days after his death, Robert Cardinal Sarah arrived at Lagrasse to attend the brother's funeral. He had known him since the autumn of 2014: we had come together to visit him. The cardinal had been impressed by his spiritual strength. I will never forget the beauty of the expression on their faces at the moment when these two men met for the first time. The cardinal came as a friend, to support a sick person and pray with him. I was also present when he entered the church where the dead man's body lay.

The emotion of the cardinal was immense. I was fortunate enough to be the enthralled witness of this story— the silent friendship between a young sick man and one of the most important prelates in the Church. Even today, it is difficult for me to think of those moments without crying.

Brother Vincent was the first to die in the community. The canons wanted to spend long moments in his presence. Father Emmanuel-Marie sent children, religious, and sick people to pray in the chapel where Brother Vincent reposed. Everyone felt an extraordinary peace and joy upon leaving the oratory where the sick man had attended Mass in the past.

On the day of his burial, solemnity and joy penetrated even the stones of the abbey. His grave had been dug two years earlier—the brothers had so often believed that they would lose him. An important crowd accompanied the young man. When the canons were closing the coffin, his mother asked to kiss him on the forehead one last time. Then the wooden lid was closed.

The climb to the cemetery affected the whole community. The long procession passed through the gardens and the avenue of olive trees. Nature was magnificent, the birds were singing, and the blue sky dazzled the canons. One day, they would walk the same path as Brother Vincent. Through him, eternal life had become tangible.

Ten days after Brother Vincent's death, Father Emmanuel-Marie was informed of inexplicable phenomena obtained through his intercession. Several terminally ill people had been suddenly cured without any medical explanation. In the medieval garden, at the apse of the abbey, a canon told me with confidence "The brother works in heaven as he did on earth, with passion, precision, and discretion. He is a saint with a method."

Today, friends and strangers come to visit Brother Vincent in the community's cemetery, which has become a pilgrimage destination. His grave is simple and modest. The tall trees, the little wooden cross, and the young boxwood are a perfect final backdrop.

Two months after the burial, Father Emmanuel-Marie organized a meeting of the whole community with a person responsible for palliative care in Montpellier. The brothers said distressing things they had never expressed before. Some of them were able to speak about their fear of death, others about the fear of illness and anxiety in the face of suffering. Some religious explained with emotion that they could no longer enter Brother Vincent's room. Through him, they also mourned other loved ones. Still others described their sadness after his departure. Some of them suspected life-prolonging treatment. On the other hand, the canons wanted to be sure that the doctors had not pushed him toward death. There are as many reactions to death as there are men.

The brother infirmarians, Brother Théophane and Brother Bernard, had great difficulty accepting his death.

The day Brother Vincent died, they were not at the abbey. For both men, it was a terrible shock. They would have liked to be present. Brother Théophane and Brother Bernard felt guilty. The two religious were so attached to him that they did not want to see him die. Brother Vincent finally understood it. He waited until they were away to leave. He knew he could not die if his guardian angels were standing near him. They would have succeeded in reviving him. In his own way, Brother Vincent had run away. After his death, his absence became all-consuming. The brother infirmarians had spent three years, night and day, with Brother Vincent. Even now, the brother's room remains unoccupied.

At the final moment, Father Emmanuel-Marie did not cry. Now when he speaks, his throat knots up. The violence of the suffering, the brevity of the life, the injustice of the death of Brother Vincent opened a chasm beneath his feet. It reminded him of the servant in Isaiah, of the lamb who would be sacrificed. Brother Vincent never raised his voice in the face of suffering. Multiple sclerosis did not get the better of his humility, his kindness, his simplicity, his greatness.

Brother Vincent is a mystery. The canons always felt he was happy. The physical suffering was terrible, unbearable, but the spiritual joy was greater. During his agony, Brother Pierre often asked him this question: "Brother Vincent, is it very difficult to bear? Do you suffer greatly?" He responded "yes" with a blink. His anxiety, his distress, his fear hurt his brothers. Physical ailments are difficult, but mental suffering is immeasurable. The obvious reality of being nothing, of losing the most fundamental abilities, is even deeper than the greatest physical wounds. At thirty-five, Brother Vincent had no more dreams.

He certainly had the feeling of having been abandoned.

Forgetfulness will perhaps sweep away Benoît Carbonell's memory. Soon, newcomers to the community will not have known him.

The canons were like children on a beach protecting a sand castle. The sea rises, and the beautiful construction is doomed. So the little ones take action with the naïveté of young pirates and the energy of those who know they will lose the battle. The inevitable happens; the water rises to the heart of the castle, and the walls of sand collapse in an instant, without making a sound. Brother Vincent was a friable castle, a castle on a scaffold. The religious who were close to him were transformed by the suffering of Brother Vincent. Fragile and nervous brothers became rocks.

The day of the funeral, Father Emmanuel-Marie addressed Brother Vincent. A simple phrase still resounds in our memories. "Your pulpit was not a pulpit but a white bed of immobility."

Brother Vincent was a giant. His body melted like the snow in the spring sunshine, but his soul was lighter every day.

He fought like a lion cub who knew the end of the battle. Savage beasts tore his muscles and broke his bones. Brother Vincent emerged victorious.

II

The Shadow of the
Black Mountain

En-Calcat Abbey

Between Castres and Carcassonne, the valleys are battered by the Autan wind. There, among imposing, late-nineteenth-century buildings, a church of dressed stone, a shaded cloister, workshops, orchards, undergrowth draw the face of a beautiful and singular abbey. Not far from there, in the countryside of the little village of Dourgne, Sainte-Scholastique is the domain of the nuns. The monastery resembles a castle of Ludwig II of Bavaria, lost in the Tarn fields and foliage.

I came to En-Calcat to meet Dom David Tardif d'Hamon-ville, the eighth Father Abbot since its founding in 1890.

The fifty Benedictines who live at En-Calcat are the spiritual sons of a master builder, Dom Romain Banquet, who willed this large monastery with all his might. Since then, despite the storms, the squalls, men have made the abbey a spiritual homeland, from novitiate to the final hours of life.

In the middle of the twentieth century, sheltered by the great walls of its enclosure, the abbey experienced a glorious period. The composer Dom Clément Jacob, Guy de Chaunac-Lanzac, one of the greatest names in contemporary tapestry making, in religion the famous Dom Robert, as well as the pianist Thierry de Brunhoff are some of the illustrious figures who have stayed at the abbey.

In this sunny countryside, vocations were numerous. Young men continue to knock at the door, but older monks form an important part of the community. A year never passes without the abbey burying several monks.

I loved En-Calcat. Every morning, at eight fifty, I heard the bells peal. Soon, daily Mass began. In the choir, the contrast was painful between the young monks and elderly brothers, with slightly lost expressions, stooped bodies, hoarse voices.

I had the same feeling in the refectory. The table of great elders moved me deeply. There were six of them. Tomorrow, perhaps, one of them will have left this earth. A monk dressed in a big white apron watched all their movements. Wedged against the back of a wheelchair, Brother Olivier was eighty-nine years old. An emaciated face, white complexion, hollow eyes, a black woolen cap on his head, he slowly swallowed his vegetable soup. At every meal, I found these men who had reached the end of the long monastic road. Their asceticism, their immobility, their weaknesses touched me.

In the church, the old monks of En-Calcat listened to the services from the gallery on the first floor, close to heaven. These Benedictines no longer sang. They simply followed the psalms in their books attentively. The brother infirmarian stayed close to them like a guardian angel. He knew word for word this passage from the rule of Saint Benedict: "Care for the sick should take precedence. We will serve them truly as Christ, who said: 'I was sick and you visited me.'"

Near the monastery, the monks' cemetery resembled an English garden. In this month of April 2017, the springtime was joyful. Scattered flowers around the tombs, tall grass in the paths, the gentleness of the sun, and the magnificent blue sky gave the enclosure of the dead an enchanting air. At the back of the garden, a craftsman was working to restore an ossuary beneath a courtyard. Below, an old monk was returning slowly from a walk; another, younger, in sportswear, was tearing across the courtyard to begin a run.

I observed the names inscribed on the little steles. They told well the history of the Benedictines of En-Calcat: Brother Lambert Kampé de Fériet, priest, died January 15, 2009, Brother Olric de Bouvier, priest, died May 27, 2009, Brother Antoine de Lambilly, priest, died November 28, 2010, Brother Marie-Bernard de Soos, priest, died March 13, 2012, Brother Victor de Champlouis, priest, died December 21, 1991, Brother Pierre de la Jonquière, priest, died February 2, 2000, Brother Bède des

Rochettes, priest, died August 17, 1998, Brother Paul-Benoît d'Azy, priest, died March 8, 2000, Brother Guy de Maurepas, priest, died October 25, 2001. And, near a tall cross, lost in the undergrowth, the enigmatic tomb of the third abbot of En-Calcat, Father Marie de Floris, died in 1994.

In a light-filled and comfortable sitting room, Dom David d'Hamonville told me without affectation about the death of his brothers. He spoke with the intelligence of an artist and the heart of a good, sensitive, and sensible man who has just lived through painful moments.

The year 2016 had been particularly difficult. Within six months, the community had accompanied six brothers on the road to the cemetery. The first week of November, the abbey lost two monks. Dom David was in Ivory Coast when, on the 26th of October, he learned of the death of brother Xavier. Then, the night of All Saints, in a terrible *crescendo*, Father Michel-Marie died in his turn.

The latter was sixty-two years old. He suffered an oligoastrocytoma, an inoperable brain tumor. He could no longer be saved, even if chemotherapy had prolonged his life for several months. Exhausted from his African voyage, Dom David returned to the abbey in the afternoon on October 31st. The patient was dying. His breathing was a battle, his face no longer had any color. The Father Abbot came to see him three times in the space of a few hours: "During the night, a monk knocked softly on the door of my cell to tell me that Father Michel-Marie was in heaven. He was freed. Still, I did not sleep that night. On November 2, in the homily for the Mass for the Dead, I recalled that in the old days, in the monasteries, one prepared a long time for death. We said that the whole monastic life was *meditatio mortis*. The role of the Father Abbot was always to encourage the old monks to face the end of the road. Today, there is no longer any question of that. At the moment when life hangs by a thread, there is the emergency medical service, the firemen, and before the day of final departure, there are many small departures in white cars or red vans; oxygen, transfusion, antibiotics, then life resumes, for a few weeks or a few short years. Why worry an elderly brother by speaking to him about the last things? When I visit a monk to tell him that heaven approaches, I have to be certain of his state of health. If not, the spiritual path no longer has meaning."

Dom David has known monks who refused death, persuaded that doctors were going to find the right cure. How can one understand the obstinacy of an elderly brother who does not want to accept the inevitable? Dom David told me of a religious who was between life and death. At any moment, he could die. His heart mysteriously continued to beat. The monk dozed for most of the day. A relative asked the monastery for treatment to delay the fatal outcome.

How could Dom David respond? The Father Abbot of En-Calcat had always believed it was not right to struggle to keep a very elderly person alive: "If a monk allows himself to be dragged into this game, he loses the meaning of his religious profession, which consists in the knowledge that we owe our lives to Another." Dom David does not trust a system where medicine alone gives meaning to life. "Where is God in these complex mechanisms?" He is afraid of this transfer from the divine to medical power.

A number of monks have died in the hospital; the brothers are no longer fools. Sometimes, economic management takes precedence over the care of the sick: "The doctors are wonderful. But they can treat us like livestock. Do they need a hospital room? The sick brother is sent back to the monastery. The day before, there was no question of a return. Our infirmarian saw an ambulance arrive without having been warned", Dom David attests. He feels uncomfortable with these questions. When a doctor calls to tell him a monk is going to leave the hospital, it is not unusual for the monk to be almost in a coma. He has little time to accompany him toward death. Before the doctor comes to recognize that he can do nothing more, the monks have lost precious time. Dom David has fought with doctors who try hard to keep the very old alive: "Shouldn't a ninety-year-old brother who suffers from terrible pneumonia return to God? I can hardly oppose a medical decision. The doctors have the power to delay the definitive meeting of a religious with his Creator. The scenario is often the same. The moment we call emergency services or the ambulance, we lose control over the patient."

En-Calcat has twenty monks over the age of eighty. Seven of them are over ninety. The doctor comes several times a week. Dom David fears the young physicians because they do not dare take risks. With them, rapid hospitalization is most often the rule. In the monastery infirmary, the atmosphere is peaceful. The doctors and nurses appreciate their visits to the abbey. They understand that the elderly brothers live there in peace. But they do not give up practices that are in contradiction with monastic life. Sometimes, the doctor is brave enough to admit that the end is near.

Listening to Dom David, I thought of the rule of Saint Benedict: the founder of monasticism reminds us that the novice will be warned "about the hard and bitter things by which one goes to God".

The Father Abbot spoke to me for a long time about Father Michel-Marie, whose death was exemplary. Despite his brain tumor, he remained joyful. Up to the end, even when his cancer had deprived him of speech, he spent long hours in prayer. He died as an obedient, faithful, and humble monk.

Father Michel-Marie was the eighth child of a beautiful family. He had been the prior, master of novices, responsible for the African foundation of En-Calcat. He was a balanced man. An engineering school graduate, tall, handsome, intelligent, he had all the qualities for success. But he preferred to become a monk. Father Michel-Marie and Dom David were together in the novitiate; they had walked together for thirty years. After Dom David was elected abbot, Father Michel-Marie was his right hand, his shield, his counselor. Father Michel-Marie had a special gift for understanding the psychological and human poverties of his peers. He knew he was free of it, but he said that those who suffered martyrdom because of their depression were very important to God. He believed sick monks were closer to heaven than healthy ones.

A year before his death, during his remission, Father Michel-Marie received a journalist. He was afraid of suffering, and yet he gave him this wonderful speech: "Knowing myself thus affected by the sickness has made me hypersensitive. I realize at what point life is not important. At the same time, it takes on all of its importance. I am now clearly aware of the end of all things. But it is necessary to get up and fight for life. I am very nervous about dying, like I was before taking an exam. The immensity of what awaits us in heaven is frightening. Yet, I have a role to play in this greatness. Here on earth, everything I do prepares what I will have to live in heaven. But this is beyond me. I have realized the incredible immensity of what waits for me on the other side." The power, the light of Dom David illuminated his funeral.

The monks prepared the remains. Dom David placed a cocoa pod between his hands, a souvenir from his life in Africa. Father Michel-Marie had brought it back from Ivory Coast. It was pressed against him when the brothers lowered his body into the grave.

In a monastery, as in regular life, the question of psychological illnesses is a subject of concern. How to help elderly monks who have become senile or to help depressed monks? How to understand their needs? In February 2017, Brother Élie died at ninety-five years of age. Prior, cellarer, he had held all the important positions at En-Calcat. In his final years, he had been huddled up in a world to which the community no longer had access. Little nods of the head took the place of sentences. Brother Élie said he had gone deaf. In reality, he heard perfectly well anything he wanted to know. The monk had walled himself up with God. He listened to the services in his room thanks to a broadcasting system. Faithful, he had recited his rosary up to his final day. After his death, Dom David read his spiritual notebook. His intimate notes revealed to him how the workings of autism had triumphed over the richness of his past life. Brother Élie was an artist and a man crushed by administrative tasks for which he was ill-suited. At sixty, when he was relieved from all his duties, he became a ceramist. Little by little, Brother Élie isolated himself without ever speaking of the suffering that had consumed him for so long. He sank into a deep depression. Dialogue with others became impossible.

Where is God in the life of monks suffering from a psychological illness? Dom David believes that it is difficult for a sick person to recover the quality of his former spiritual life. The psychological troubles that affect the brothers become a kind of barrier, a sign on which would be written in capital letters "PLEASE DO NOT ENTER": "I do not want to remain silent about this reality that affects all monasteries", Dom David told me, "this refusal to speak, this distaste for divine realities." In the dark forests of apathy, monastic life is reduced to its most simple material aspect. The Liturgy of the Hours is a shadow, a path of brambles, a long suffocation. No one even knows if the sick monks still hear the beautiful ringing of the bells.

The great trial of En-Calcat was the suicide of a forty-eight-year-old monk. In April 2012, on Easter Tuesday, Brother Irénée took his life by taking sleeping pills. He was a brother infirmarian. It took the monks a while to find his body. They spent an entire day, without rest, looking for him. On the little table in his cell, a word jotted on a piece of paper left no doubt for the reason of his absence.

Brother Irénée had entered the monastery at thirty. The young religious had a suicidal past known to some of his old friends. A few months before the tragedy, he had written to one of them. Brother Irénée said that he had all the necessary medications in his infirmary to commit the irreparable. Every week, the monk went to Toulouse for psychotherapy. On that sad spring night, he never returned.

Wednesday morning, around six o'clock, the brother who worked with him realized he had not returned. Alerted, Dom David went to his cell. He found a small card. "Sorry, sorry, sorry, I am suffering too much, I am going ..." Brother Irénée was addressing his family and community for the last time. He did not blame anyone, but he wanted to die. In the pocket of his habit, the monks found a little note. He had composed a prayer to God before giving up his life to despair. "Lord, Lord, you will forgive me, I cannot go on. I cannot stay. I know that I am going to you."

Brother Irénée had gone up to the chapel of Saint-Ferréol. The little building overlooks the monastery at the summit of Black Mountain. For a long time, it has been a pilgrimage site. The novices come to walk and pray on these heights after Sunday lunch.

Near the lifeless body, the monks found a bag of medications. Tuesday evening, Brother Irénée had remained alone. Night fell, and the walkers deserted the place. From the heights, he saw his monastery. He could imagine what the monks were doing at that exact hour.

Dom David modestly and realistically described those somber days to me. His courage, his sensitivity, his humanity had to be admired. Listening to him, I could not help but think of Baudelaire's sad verses in "Spleen LXXVIII". The words came back to me like pounding in my head:

> When the low, heavy sky weighs like a lid
> Upon the spirit moaning in ennui,
> And when, spanning the circle of the world,
> It pours a black day sadder than our nights.[1]

Five years after the death of Brother Irénée, the sadness, the suffering, and the doubts were still intense. Dom David, in a voice weak as a spring that dries up in the aridity of summer, was kind enough to revisit those dark hours: "Brother Irénée committed suicide on the summit of the mountain. He went to sleep, curled up at the foot of the chapel. There was a macabre staging to his death. Wednesday morning, we had followed his trail to Toulouse. He had left an address on his table. But there was no one at the indicated place. Then we decided to inform

---

[1] Charles Baudelaire, "Spleen (IV)", in *The Flowers of Evil*, trans. James McGowan (Oxford: Oxford University Press, 2008), 149.

the police. The officers advised me to ask to locate him through his cell phone. Shortly after, someone on retreat, out walking, discovered his body."

Dom David was struggling to catch his breath. His words faltered, they stayed stuck in his throat: "I wrote the death announcement without hiding the truth. I was surprised by the messages sent to me by abbots who had lived through the same experience." Dom David paused for a long time, his gaze lost in the distance, then he continued: "The community was struck in the heart by the violence of this departure. But we were carried by the power of Holy Week, which we had just celebrated. The monks had an extraordinary awakening of faith. We wanted to stay united. They prayed a lot for me. The brothers saw the abyss into which I had fallen. I became the abbot of a religious who had chosen to kill himself. My suffering was deep, difficult, long. When we found his body, the police took the corpse for a few hours for forensic identification. I did not have the strength to go identify him."

Brother Irénée was buried shortly after Easter, Saturday *in albis*. The celebrants wore white liturgical vestments, according to the customs of this season and the wishes of the deceased. Those who attended were numerous and reverent. The monk had just given up a professorship at the Catholic Institute of Toulouse, where he taught Hebrew. His friends and students came to bid him farewell.

Brother Irénée left carrying the key to his mystery, his impulses, his pain. He was buried in the cemetery of the monks. On a small stone placed on the earth, the inscription is solemn: "F. Irénée—April 11, 2012."

The abbey had to rebuild its faith. The monks had no choice but to accept the humiliation of a scathing denial; only prayer remained for moving forward. Exhausted, Dom David had to find the strength to support a monk close to Brother Irénée. He left the monastery six months after the suicide. He was then in the clutches of a violent depression. The abbey had initiated a process of secularization. The religious who returned to the world had been the only one to receive a letter of farewell from Brother Irénée. He could not leave without giving him the reasons for his action. From then on, the former monk returned to the abbey for funerals or monastic professions.

Still today, Dom David is trying to understand Brother Irénée's action: "The dramatic aspect of our brother's suicide shows the presence of the Evil One. In deciding to leave on the day after Easter, Brother Irénée knew he was choosing an important date. He was adding additional violence to his death. We were annihilated. Did he want to make us suffer? He had cried out, but we could no longer respond. Where is the monastery where a monk does not encounter psychological problems? Men enter at twenty, and they are supposed to pass sixty years of an intense and demanding monastic life. The monks change, their world views become more complex. With time, the ardors of those first years fade. Some sufferings become unbearable."

Dom David has never forgotten Father Damien. The monk died three years after his arrival. He always knew him to be affected by a mental illness. In the halls or the cloister, he fought against an imaginary demon, his body twisted by large striking gestures. Young, he was full of hope. Good and pious, he possessed all the monastic qualities. The photos from that time show a religious with a smiling face. He had the confidence of children who know they are safe. One day, bent under accumulated fatigue, Father Damien suffered a psychological crash. The obsessions, the paranoia, the delirium, his troubles, little by little, became a permanent state. For a long time, he was interned in a psychiatric home. After many infernal nights, many empty days, many tears, the doctors thought that he should return to the monastery. The Father Abbot studied his history; he knew that Father Damien had a true vocation. But the machine had stopped; it was impossible to go back.

Dom David d'Hamonville believes that monasteries have always welcomed men who have a hard time living. The thirst for God is sometimes overwhelmed by existential evils. The origin of a vocation could be an immature disinterest in the things of the world or emotional and social wounds. But, without the desire to seek God, a man is incapable of walking for long on the path of religious life. "The monks who do well are those who know that we are all a little damaged. In a monastery, we often have a little account to settle with normality", the Father Abbot confided in me.

There is another evil of the mind, difficult and terrible, of which we spoke with sadness. Two Benedictines at En-Calcat were stricken with Alzheimer's at the same time. Father Efflam and Brother Joseph showed different symptoms. Their memories burned progressively, but the flames were not the same.

Brother Joseph became incapable of holding a conversation. He no longer knew his own name or those of others. For his part, Father Efflam no longer had control of the threads of his own life, but he had not forgotten anything about those of others. He remained capable of having endless discussions about the history of France and the geography of some distant country.

The two men spent their days together. Alone, they were lost, disoriented, unhappy. But when the brother infirmarian placed the hand of one in that of the other, they would go for a walk together on the little paths that

surrounded the monastery. In church, Father Efflam and
Brother Joseph were recollected, focused. They resembled
children learning to pray. In the afternoon, they sat beside
each other, always in the same place, and they talked for
hours, about everything and nothing.

One winter morning, Father Efflam was found dead in
his bed. For Brother Joseph, it was a terrible blow. His
companion in illness had caught a mild cold. He departed
in his sleep, like a feather falling to the ground without
making a sound.

In the last photos, Father Efflam had the look of a happy
and distracted child. The monks of En-Calcat liked to say
that his old age was a return to the maternal breast. The
torments of the disease did not get the better of his purity,
his candor, his fragility, his smile. Certainly, he was no
longer in control of his life. The infirmarians and the community decided everything for him. But he remained full
of wonder.

Father Efflam lived the monastic way perfectly. The
monks who knew him do not know if they could be so
obedient to the will of God. Dom David had no doubt: "If
Father Efflam lived with Alzheimer's disease in joy, it was
because of the simplicity of his life of prayer."

The death of the fourth Father Abbot of En-Calcat, December 13, 2010, left a mark on the memories of the monks.
Father Dominique Hermand was also suffering from Alzheimer's disease. From 1965 to 1978, his years as abbot were
difficult. In those stormy years when the winds of protest
were blowing, he accompanied seventeen brothers to the
door of the monastery. The monks left without returning.
He narrowly avoided a split within the community. How
could a man complete, with perfect joy, such a heavy existence, a life of trials that was not without sorrows?

In the final months, he marveled at everything. The wind that pushed the clouds, the avenue of plane trees, the sunlight in the refectory, the peace of the infirmary, the trees in the cloister, everything took on an extraordinary appearance. Father Dominique had a deep affection for the community when he could have pulled away from it.

Dom David was present on the day of his death. He has not forgotten that extraordinary moment. His features were tense, painful, contracted by the final efforts of his facial muscles. Breathing became difficult, gasping, suffocating. His heart was beating less and less strongly. His face changed from one moment to the next. He died smiling. Dom David's emotion remains intact: "I felt the presence of God when looking at the smile of Father Dominique as he died."

The brother infirmarians made the funerary preparations, and the body was placed in the oratory of the dead. The hours passed, he became more and more beautiful. Father Abbot asked for a brother to take a photo. His predecessor had the radiance, the smile, the perfect joy of monks. In the church, during the funeral, the religious, the priests, and the faithful could see the radiant face of the deceased. He kept that expression up to the moment when the brothers placed the pall over the body. Then they lowered his remains, without a coffin, into the open ground.

Several monks told me that death masks were changeable. There were brothers who lived like saints whose faces in death were not beautiful; others had more uneven lives, and their final expression was radiant.

The growing difficulties with hospital services do worry the monks. En-Calcat is primarily concerned about the problem of the scarcity of care in rural areas. Dom David sees the medical desert surrounding the monastery with apprehension. "In the rural world, the system of young replacement doctors has become a weak point. These new physicians do not know us. I was reassured by our old doctors who treated us for many years. Sometimes, when one of them leaves, we lose forty years' worth of familial support. They knew about the psychologies, the fears, the weaknesses. The old system was human."

I was appalled by the violent and distressing description that Dom David gave me of his dealings with the French healthcare system. The example of Father Patrice, who died in December 2016, at ninety-nine and eleven months of age, is terrible. He had been the creator of the abbey's famous zither workshop—in forty years, En-Calcat made thousands of instruments, dispersed to the four corners of the world. At the end of his life, the strength of his voice could still surpass the whole abbey choir. Father Patrice did not want to die before celebrating his hundredth birthday. The monks had planned some beautiful festivities. A month before the celebrations, they had to cancel everything. Father Patrice was hospitalized for two months in Castres for a pulmonary infection. When he at last came back among his brothers, the professor announced that he was cured. Father Patrice died two days later ... The doctors had defeated the famous bacteria they had relentlessly pursued in his lungs. But the poor man had become a weak and emaciated little fledgling. He was so thin that his pacemaker was visible beneath his pale skin. The brothers wondered if the doctors had tried new medications without informing them. This fierceness in eliminating a bacterium seemed suspicious. Had Father Patrice's flesh been used experimentally? How does one resist the authority of a medical decision that drops like an axe? Is it even possible? The elderly are without defenses. It is necessary to fight to get access to the information in medical records.

The hospitals have profitability requirements that make one shudder, and the patients are downgraded.

Dom David has spent a long time considering these questions: "Our connection with medicine has greatly evolved. There is now preventative work that did not exist before. When I entered the abbey, the monks rarely went to the infirmary. Regular checkups can save a life. In cardiology, these visits are essential. In 2010, during a simple consultation, they discovered I had coronary stenosis; the treatment saved me from a lot of problems. Though, in heaven, I would be happier. By relentlessly repairing the living, like robots, we will end up in tatters. When we put a pacemaker in a brother with Alzheimer's disease, we are caring for the heart in order to prolong the disease of the brain. Often, we have to choose between cancer, a stroke, or a heart attack. I very much enjoyed reading the philosopher Günther Anders' book *L'Obsolescence de l'homme* (The Obsolescence of man).[2] He talks about the promethean shift that marks the postmodern world. Man has created a technological world that humiliates him and makes him feel ashamed. Machines are more perfect than the human being. In this system, the error is necessarily man. Technology cannot be at fault. In contrast, in classical anthropology, man was the summit of the animal kingdom. Over the past fifty years, he has become the low point in a world dominated by technological idols. We are reduced to the role of the weak link in a system we have freely created. In a hospital, healing follows the same logic. The patient is a machine. Surgeons repair a liver, a kidney, a heart, a stomach, until the machine is so worn-out that it has to be thrown in the trash. This phenomenon affects

---

[2] Günther Anders, *L'Obsolescence de l'homme* (Paris: Fario, 2011).

Western societies, and the monks are no exception. In
opposition to this vision, I believe very much in the bib-
lical approach of the dynamism of the soul. We have to
stay in touch with God, from whom we get our breath.
This link cannot be broken. The doctor provides care,
but it is the patient who heals. The restoration of the
body is always connected with the One who gives life."

Since the election of Dom David in 2009, twenty-two
brothers have died. For the Benedictines of En-Calcat,
it is important not to forget the dead. The Father Abbot
gives the greatest care to the writing of the biographical
notes of the deceased brothers. The living try to summa-
rize the essence of the lives of the departed. In Chapter,
each monk shares his memories. The work of memory is
essential. Why speak of the dead? To make them known.
Every ten years, in the refectory, the brothers reread the
monastery's death records. The abbey has had 170 monks
die since its founding. It is necessary to fight against forgetfulness, against closing cases without further action.
The modern world consumes the living and throws them
away. The youngest ones told me they were very moved
by hearing the obituaries.

   In the Middle Ages, the abbeys possessed the famous
scroll of the dead. The parchment, on which were written
the names of the dead, was carried from one monastery to
another. A monk from Cluny traveled all over announcing the dead and calling for prayer. He added to the scroll
the names of the latest departed. Benedictine abbeys have
always cultivated the memory of the deceased. A monk
is always the inheritor of a great tradition. Saint Benedict
himself is a successor of Cassian, Basil, and Augustine.

   These practices are devoid of morbid impulses. In
Chapter, Dom David refrains from giving overly regular
news of the state of health of the elderly. Monks are in the

monastery to live. The conditions of great old age must be accepted. Brother Olivier may disappear from one day to the next, but he has his rightful place in the refectory. The novices share in serving the elderly. The young monks have a special place next to those who will soon depart. In the beginning, they are tongue-tied. They are always afraid of meeting the lifeless look of a bedridden brother.

The man who consecrates his life to God can fear the end of the road. He stalls in front of the door of the brothers staying in the infirmary. The struggle exists; it is useless to hide it.

Dom David inspires admiration because he looks truth in the face. He knows from experience that the selfishness, cowardice, and fear of one who suffers are always lurking in a corner of our heart. Suffering reveals to everyone his limits. Laymen, like monks, can become dwarfs or giants.

No one chooses his end. And yet, God allows doctors to shorten lives. When I asked Dom David about this subject, a silence came over the room where we had been speaking for so many hours: "Today, the problem of sedation is serious. We have to fight against intolerable sufferings. But if we do not feel pain anymore, life goes away. Now, with the progress of analgesics, we no longer feel anything. We no longer feel life. We no longer feel humanity. We no longer feel God approaching. Man becomes an abstract machine. Several brothers wanted to write instructions for the end of life. They refuse life-prolonging interventions, and they do not want deep sedation. We would all like to die in our sleep. The doctors induce artificial comas to be certain that the patient does not suffer anymore. Fear is a bad counselor. It is the ultimate antithesis of faith. Our materialist societies have an irrepressible obsession with pain. Why has our world forgotten that life does not exist without suffering? In the West, we are well-off, and we have trouble imagining the daily lives of the vast majority of mankind. How should I react when a ninety-year-old monk asks for a hearing aid? How should I react when this investment of three thousand euros could help twenty people in an African village? How should I react when a ninety-five-year-old brother asks for new dentures? When you consider we eat mostly eggs, fish, and little meat ... There are hypochondriac monks. These are weaknesses. If a brother agrees to work on this weakness, a big step is made. His fault is shocking, but God pardons everything." So does Dom David. His patience is immense.

En-Calcat is an oasis that one leaves with regret. To remember that time, it is enough for me to listen to Dom David one last time. In 1986, when he returned to the abbey after a first unsuccessful attempt, he had the sense of being in mourning. The young brother entered into monastic life in order to be as close as possible to the cross. He did not leave a love-interest behind him, and yet, it took him a year to regain interior joy. Every brother experiences, in his own way, a widowhood.

Entering a monastery is the first step toward death. Every day, Dom David reflects on his last hour: "When I am face to face with the Grim Reaper, I might not have the courage to look at him. But I do not see him as a threat. Death is a passage toward Christ. I hope that the son of God will come to take me by the hand. There is a Hindu allegory about the last moments that I particularly like. It distinguishes young monkeys from kittens. The latter wait without doing anything for their mother to take them in her mouth, while the little monkeys cling to their mother in order to go from branch to branch ... At the hour of death, the monk would like to be a kitten carried in the mouth of Christ."

III

A Fortress Away from the World

Solesmes Abbey

I arrived at Solesmes on June 1, 2017. The heat of an early summer overpowered the village and surrounding areas. A few minutes after having passed through the abbey gates, while speaking with the father guestmaster, I heard the sound of a death knell. It was announcing the death of Brother Pierre Buisson, an old monk who had died in his ninety-ninth year.

Shortly after, Dom Philippe Dupont came to welcome me. The Father Abbot of Solesmes is an influential person in the Catholic Church, a man well known for his culture, experience, and simplicity. Coming toward me at a brisk pace, he called out with disconcerting lightness: "We offer you a dead man!" The stage for my trip was strangely set. But I could hardly complain. I had come to Solesmes to talk about the last things.

The bells rang for twenty long minutes. With exquisite kindness and politeness, Father Bruno Lutz led me to my room. I did not wait long in the little cell that had been assigned to me. I wanted to walk around the monastery to immerse myself in the atmosphere that reigned there when it had just lost one of its sons.

The Benedictines of Solesmes are used to the overwrought descriptions of visitors who discover the majestic walls where they have chosen to pass their lives. Situated along the banks of the Sarthe, the monastery complex has an extraordinary appearance. The church dates back to the eleventh century. It houses two groups of statues called the "Saints of Solesmes". The entombment of the Virgin faces that of Christ. The multitude of people with solemn faces around the heavenly dead, the beauty of their features, the gracefulness of their figures are fascinating.

Nestled against the abbey church, the eighteenth-century priory in tuffeau stone is elegant and understated. The Maurist cloister from the same era, the huge, nineteenth-century Melet building, which houses the refectory, the large, twentieth-century cloister, with finely chiseled column capitals that the changing light never ceases to show in a new perspective, and the library, which numbers over two hundred thousand volumes, create a harmonious, solid, and radiant monastery.

The stones do not sum up the monks. These men are right to contest the grand images that have led to the creation of the Solesmesian myth. All abbeys want to be great, contemplative boats launched toward heaven. The Benedictines who pray, sing, and work at Solesmes seek God just as do the sons of Saint Benedict from the humblest of priories in an isolated area. Death is the same in a Sarthe fortress as it is in the little cells of an African monastery. God does not differentiate between them.

Brother Buisson had died in the early afternoon. Despite his departure, I had the impression that the Benedictines continued to attend to their daily tasks.

The cemetery, near an old greenhouse, was deserted. Among the graves of the monks, I noticed that of Prince Xavier of Bourbon, Duke of Parma, who died in 1977. He was the brother of Empress Zita, a great friend of the nuns of Solesmes. I followed my path toward the landscaped gardens below the abbey. The well-cut paths smelled of roses. Near a long gardeners' house, a retreatant was smoking a pipe and reading Thomas Merton. A little farther, seated around small tables, some English students, stylish and focused, were going over their exams. The bucolic and mild day seemed to ward off death, who had just knocked on the door of the place.

Built facing the bakery and the Grand Hotel, the abbey is situated in the center of a peaceful town. Solesmes is a perfect image of a tranquil France. The streets are calm and wise. At the end of the main thoroughfare, on the other side of the bridge that spans the Sarthe, I found the famous view of the abbey. The image of a rich and powerful monastery, renowned the world over.

Near the road that runs along the river, walkers suddenly rushed to find shelter. Dark clouds were gathering in the sky. Wind was blowing in the tall trees on the languid banks. The monastic fortress was changing color. The shimmering, romantic façades were becoming sad walls the color of soot.

Around four o'clock, I returned to the monastery. The storm had burst. In one corner of the cemetery, two young monks armed with heavy shovels were just beginning to dig a grave. The exercise was physical. The religious did not seem discouraged by the work ahead of them. After each office, the pile of earth grew next to the grave.

In a little while, I would be talking with Father Jean-Philippe Lemaire. Several monks had warned me. I should prepare myself to meet a saint.

For a long time, Father Jean-Philippe held the highest office at Solesmes. Sickness and old age led him to give up his responsibilities. His face is pale and his gaze envelops his interlocutors with an infinite sweetness.

Thin, hunched, he never mentions the double scoliosis that causes him great suffering. With a touching modesty, he speaks about his role with the sick: "I am the spare wheel for my biological brother, Father Joseph-Michel Lemaire. He is the infirmarian of the monastery." Five monks work regularly with him. Since he left his position as prior, Father Jean-Philippe helps them. In particular, he takes care of a severely handicapped brother.

The monk in question is not very old. He just celebrated his eighty-second birthday: "Father Bernard Andry was the sub-prior of our Palendriai foundation in Lithuania. In six years, he lost all his intellectual faculties. We organized his return with care. Father Bernard entered the monastery in 1954. Joyful, mischievous, warm, he was the principal cantor for many years. Today, he is totally dependent. We have to feed him, get him up, and put him to bed. Every morning, I see to getting him dressed. No one knows if he understands what we say to him. The doctors cannot diagnosis it for certain as Alzheimer's disease. Specialists have the greatest difficulty defining this kind of cerebral degeneration. Father Bernard does not receive any treatment. At mealtimes, he swallows an analgesic. I could not tell you if he is suffering. Sometimes, I notice a grimace on his face that seems to indicate pain. Our brother is an invalid full of kindness. Physically, he is still strong. When he shakes your hand, he is capable of breaking your palm. He has more energy than I do." I should say that Father Jean-Philippe is seventy-nine years old, the age of his patients: "My weakness allows me to understand the sick better. I know suffering, and I understand the burdens of age. In the evenings, putting Father Andry to bed takes more than twenty minutes. There is a temptation to give care quickly. When we repeat such difficult tasks over so many years, how can we avoid a kind of dehumanized routine? Seeking to save time, we transform the sick person into a poor object. I need to be attentive so as not to rush through my work in order to flee to other, more rewarding occupations. If you look after a patient going to bed two hundred times a year, it is difficult to maintain the same attentiveness as during the early days. We are not looking to avoid the facts. The infirmary monks need to be vigilant so as not to transform a brother into a thing they take care of mechanically and as quickly as possible. The risk of commodification of the sick exists. I must pray to keep the strength of my desire to serve awake. Father Andry is Christ. When we come before God, we will be accountable for our charity toward the weakest. I need to know how to lose my time for the sick. In life, giving freely is essential. Christ said that the man who loses his life gains it. When I enter the room, I stroke his hand to revive our brotherhood; and I tell him: 'Ah, Brother Bernard, you are my brother, my beloved brother, my big brother!'"

The monks do not know if Father Andry understands them. They want to believe that the patient makes use of a faculty of comprehension mysterious in the eyes of men: "The days when we take him to recreation and the monks laugh, he bursts out laughing. Is it simple mimicry or a desire to have fun? A few months ago, he responded 'yes' to the question of a brother infirmarian. I suspect he understands certain things. I know almost nothing about his life of prayer. I try to lead him often to the chapel in the infirmary. I tell him: 'Brother Bernard, I am leaving you in front of the tabernacle. Jesus is there.' Then I say a Hail Mary. The prayer helps me not to become an automaton. In his little chair, he stays a moment in the chapel. When Mass is celebrated in the oratory, I always come with Father Bernard. He no longer receives Communion since we do not know if he is cognizant. But I place the rosary in his hands. He does not say a single word."

The words of Father Jean-Philippe are a reflection of his greatness of spirit. I understood that he was filled with wonder at all the patients in his charge. Father Pierre Estorges, ninety-one years old, is one of them. This monk has been blind for almost thirty years. He has refused to eat for several months. Should the infirmarians respect a decision that would slowly kill him? The only action he can still do alone is drink. Father Pierre is easy, simple, he never complains. His brothers do not know if he still distinguishes what he eats. The invalid opens his mouth like an infant and swallows the spoonful the infirmarians give him. Every monk has a different relationship with suffering. Some are sensitive; others demonstrate an incredible strength. Telling me about Father Pierre, my interlocutor wondered: "People who have never known suffering should avoid speaking to those who experience it. Suffering is a great mystery. It is always unpleasant. The monk offers himself to God to pray, and he gives his life to the Church. The final step, even if in fear, is desired and known. The monk, remains completely a man, and he reaches out toward the divine."

Decades later, some deaths still raise questions and heartache. Father Jean-Phillipe has not forgotten anything about the day of May 30, 1961. That day, Brother Roland du Bourblanc died at the age of nineteen. He was in the novitiate, having just received the habit. After having served Mass, Brother Roland left for the refectory to have breakfast. There, he dropped dead. Father Jean-Philippe arrived shortly after. He noticed that Brother Roland had not eaten his bread. When he left, headed toward the sacristy, he asked a monk where Brother Roland was. He told him that the young monk had gone to heaven. The doctors suspected a heart defect. The memories of the old monk come rushing back: "October 7, 1958, when I entered Solesmes, I was struck by the joy that inhabited the monastery at the time of deaths. In civil life, I was used to mourning, tears, black. In our abbey, I understood that death was simple and uneventful. Certainly, Christ cried at the death of Lazarus. But in a house of God, we do not cry. The monk spends his life desiring heaven. I often think of Father Paul, who was a great theologian. When the Father Abbot came see him in his room, he exclaimed: 'I am at peace. In a few hours, I will see God. How thrilling!' We should be happy for our brothers who are arriving at the gates of Paradise. The one great desire of a monk is to ascend to heaven. Human reflexes exist: we can be sad at the thought of waiting a long time before meeting again those whom we love. However, the joy is stronger. Our burials are happy. In the cemetery, we do not have the feeling of a goodbye. It is a little step before eternity. The monastery is the antechamber of a great happiness. Monks often die in small groups. Solesmes goes through long periods without deaths, then several group departures. It is the will of God. The Father calls when he wills. But from an arithmetical perspective, there is a general rule."

My day ended with Compline. Every evening, the monks sing a hymn asking God to banish night terrors: "Procul recedant somnia, et noctium phantasmata" (Let the dreams and phantoms of the night flee far away). Brother Pierre Buisson did not have need of this prayer. He would never again have bad dreams. For several hours, his sleep had been eternal. I crossed the gardens to return to the church. The wind played in the flowering linden trees. The smell of geraniums, the well-trimmed boxwood in the French-style gardens—time seemed frozen. The noise of the world was already a distant memory.

The nave of the abbey church resembles a long ship, narrow and dark. It opens into the magnificent gothic choir in which the sixteenth-century stalls are a masterpiece of the last French Renaissance.

Near the entrance, a monk was ringing the bells to announce the final office. I seated myself on one of the benches reserved for those making retreats. The atmosphere was recollected and serious. A little bell sounded. It was calling each person away from his personal prayer. The procession of monks slowly extended to the center of the sanctuary.

Then I saw the novices who were carrying on their shoulders the open casket of Brother Pierre. The young monks who were beginning their monastic lives were carrying the old brother who had left the world.

The white, wooden coffin, of great simplicity, had been made by the monastery's brother cabinetmaker. The novices placed it on the floor in the middle of the stalls. They placed at its foot a candle and a bouquet of multi-colored roses, freshly gathered from the garden. The brother's body was facing the altar. His hood had been raised over his head, and he held a rosary in his hands. He held a large wooden cross on his chest.

A deathly silence filled the whole church. The monks said the first words of an office that the deceased had recited thousands of times throughout his life. I observed the Father Abbot. He was collected and dignified. The luminous gravity of his furrowed face reminded me of the seventeenth-century portraitists, particularly Philippe de Champaigne.

I remembered his respectful and sensitive manner speaking about a monk whom he loved: "I always ask my brothers to die when I am at the abbey. I travel a lot because of my duties as superior of the congregation of Solesmes. Brother Pierre Buisson did not want to reach one hundred. So, I knew that time was running out. For several weeks, he had been declining. At the end of the month of May, when I left for Spain, I asked him to wait for my return to die. He obeyed me. Returning to the abbey, I went quickly to his room. We were on the brink of his death. He went out like a little flame. He said that his suitcase was ready. Up until the end, Brother Pierre spent hours in prayer. He visited the cemetery every day to honor the dead. He never spoke ill of anyone. Our brother left before the office of Sext, while the infirmarian had briefly left to prepare an IV. I went to give him absolution." The Father Abbot was happy and peaceful. He had been able to see him one last time. He could not imagine being absent from Solesmes at such special moments as these.

Upon leaving, some monks looked at the body. Others preferred to lower their eyes. Brother Pierre Buisson would spend the night at the church in his coffin, watched over by the religious one at a time, surrounded by vigilant and affectionate prayer; in his day, he had kept watch near all his dead brothers.

The old monk had the face and hands of a wax figure. He resembled a praying child, confident and naïve, a slight smile at the corner of his lips, a happy smile.

Outside the sun was setting. The birds were no longer singing in the tress; the storm had started again, and the breeze was weaving through the pathways. Far off, along the Sarthe, thunder rumbled. A young religious was praying alone in the cemetery as the rain fell loudly on the sheet metal covering the grave that awaited the body of Brother Pierre.

Walking toward my cell, I saw on a little bench the bouquets of lilies that a brother gardener had carefully prepared for the burial the following day.

The day of June 3rd began with Matins, followed by Lauds. These long prayers were the two last offices sung in the presence of Brother Pierre. The silence settled again when the community left the choir. An old Benedictine came for a moment of reflection near the body. He approached slowly, recited a prayer, and retreated. All the lights were extinguished except for the candle of the deceased.

Brother Buisson had passed the baton. From now on, he was a part of Solesmes from above. The torch that burned in front of his body resembled all those he had carried since 1949—when he was eighteen, with his whole life ahead of him. Now, he was passing on this flame to the community. I had the feeling that he wanted them to carry it with courage and perseverance.

In small groups, the monks came to pray their breviaries. Outside, near the sacristy, old Brother Rémy was lovingly taking care of the geraniums. An agreeable odor of wet soil rose from the ground.

At eleven fifteen A.M., the death knell sounded again. The church filled little by little. A novice arranged candles in the stalls. Another extinguished the candle placed in front of the coffin. The procession of celebrants left the sacristy and went up quickly toward the choir. In front of the deceased, the choristers intoned the Requiem chant: "Requiam aeternam dona eis, Domine, et lux perpetua luceat eis" (Give them eternal rest, Lord, and let perpetual light shine upon them).

The Father Abbot was seated on an episcopal throne of wrought iron. He wore a magnificent Art Deco chasuble designed by an artist monk of Solesmes, Dom Henri de Laborde. Two novices were seated on the floor at his feet. One carried the crozier, and the other the miter.

The Mass was simple. The big organ remained silent. Dom Dupont did not give a homily or a eulogy. The monks had written a simple and uplifting obituary, placed in the church pews: "Born in Paris on January 24, 1919, to Victor Buisson and Marthe Sureau, baptized the following March 23 at Saint Lambert's parish and confirmed June 13, 1929, in the chapel of Notre-Dame-de-la-Salette, Pierre Robert Buisson took the habit at Solesmes on September 12, 1947, made his first vows February 11, 1950, on the feast of Our Lady of Lourdes, and his solemn profession three years later on the same date. For as long as his strength permitted, he worked in the abbey sewing room, where monastic habits are made and repaired. Very helpful and even-tempered, a man of prayer very attached to the Divine Office, he won the esteem and affection of everyone."

The offertory hymn was beautiful, slow, and solemn: "Domine Iesu Christe, Rex Gloriae, libera animas omnium fidelium defunctorum....":

Lord Jesus Christ, King of glory, deliver the souls of all the faithful departed from the pains of hell and the deep abyss;

deliver them from the lion's jaws, so that the abyss will not
swallow them, so that they will not fall into darkness; but
so that the standard-bearer Saint Michael will bring them
to the holy light that you once promised to Abraham and
his posterity. Behold, Lord, our sacrifices and our prayers
offered to your praise; accept them for these souls whom
we remember today. Lord, let them pass from death to
the life you once promised to Abraham and his posterity.

The Mass proceeded like all the others at which the
deceased had assisted. After Communion, I was struck by
the look full of friendship and tenderness of an old brother,
as he passed near the coffin.

Brother Buisson was a quiet person. In the final weeks,
he had daily nausea. He could hardly eat anymore. His life
had become difficult, but he bore it without complaining. He remained simple and good. The monks could not
count how many dozens of rosaries he was able to say each
day. At the end, he was always thirsty. When the infirmarians helped him to drink a glass of water, he thanked them
abundantly. But he was waiting for death. Father Pierre
said: "It's not right, it's not right, I have to leave." The
religious died suddenly. He prayed God would call him
home. He was answered.

The Mass ended, the liturgy displayed its final lights.
The funeral rites of the Church are an inverted mirroring
of the first actions of a midwife who swaddles a newborn
who has just left its mother's womb. The monks are committed to giving the dead the same care they received from
the woman who opened them to life.

At Solesmes, for funerals, all the monks leave in procession to the cemetery holding large, lit candles in their
hands. They sing the hymn "In paradisum": "In paradisum
deducant te angeli, in tua adventu suscipiant te martyres, et

perducant te in civitatem sanctam Ierusalem" (May choirs of angels escort you into Paradise: and at your arrival, may the martyrs receive you and welcome you; may they bring you home into the holy city, Jerusalem.)

The novices and the father infirmarian carried the coffin one last time. They crossed the nave with measured steps. From the retreatants' pews, I could see the face of the deceased, who was slowly moving away. I had the impression that he was looking one last time at the vaulted ceiling that had carried his prayer. When the coffin passed under the doorway, the emotion was strong. The monks returned to the church. For Brother Pierre, everything was finished in this valley of tears.

The procession left the abbey. The wind picked up. The monks headed toward the cemetery, where they arranged themselves in two long lines. The Father Abbot came to the foot of the coffin. He incensed it for a long time. Then the father infirmarian brought a board to close the large box. The novices quickly lowered the coffin. The Father Abbot was standing closest to the grave. He was the first to bless the grave, soon followed by all the monks.

In the wide lane that bordered the church, Dom Philippe Dupont greeted the family with kindness. Brother Buisson was old. He had few relatives. But his nephews and his nieces who were present that day were deeply moved. The monks slowly entered the sacristy. The funeral was over. The rain started again. Brother Pierre was in heaven.

During the lunch that followed, the obituary of the day spoke of Dom Antony Bonnet, who had died in 1990. *Recto tono*, a monk described his heroic captivity in Germany during the Second World War, his musical talent, and his sudden death. The monks listened in silence. They sang the benediction and left the refectory, passing by the enormous double chimney.

In the early afternoon, two monks came to fill in the grave. The little storm that was blowing did not make their task any easier. In work clothes, armed with their famous shovels, they were orderly and meticulous. When their work was done, they placed a small bouquet of red and yellow flowers and foliage on the grave. I could not help thinking of the verses of Victor Hugo:

> And when I come, I'll place upon your tomb
> Some flowering heather and a holly spray.[1]

For the monks of Solesmes, the death of a very old monk is not an ordeal. Dom Philippe Dupont confided in me with unaffected certitude: "At Solesmes, death is peaceful. With age, the monks become holy. I think of our good Father Joseph Gajard. He was afraid of death. God allowed him to overcome his anxiety. He died simply. He was resting in his room. For two days, he had felt tired. Father Joseph departed like a candle. A little breeze came to collect his soul. I realized that the monks of Solesmes were leaving quickly, unpredictably. I am certain that Brother Pierre Buisson is in heaven and that he is happy." In the church, the brothers were installing a large carpet in the choir for the feast of Pentecost. Life was renewing its usual course at Solesmes.

Every evening, after Compline, Dom Philippe Dupont goes down into the crypt that is situated under the abbey choir. In these sacred depths are buried the former Father Abbots of Solesmes. Since the resumption of Benedictine

---

[1] Victor Hugo, "Demain, dès l'aube, à l'heure où blanchit la compagne ...", in *Selected Poems of Victor Hugo*, trans. E. H. and A. M. Blackmore (Chicago: Chicago University Press, 2001), 199.

life, in 1833, there have been six in succession. Dom Prosper Guéranger, the illustrious restorer, who marked the French spiritual life of the nineteenth century, Dom Charles Couturier, the zealous successor, Dom Paul Delatte, a brilliant intellect and great theologian, Dom Germain Cozien, tenacious and courageous, Dom Jean Prou, craftsman of the conciliar *aggiornamento*, and, since 1992, Dom Philippe Dupont. The latter kneels at the precise spot where he will be buried: "I come to pray to our founder, so that he may help me in my task and watch over the salvation of my soul."

Dom Philippe remembers with precision the magnificent departure of his predecessor: "In November 1999, as a community we lived through the death of the Father Abbot emeritus Jean Prou. His dying lasted longer than usual in our abbey. He received the sacrament of the sick in front of all the monks gathered in his cell. The day before his death, we recited the prayer of the dying. He spoke to ask the brothers for forgiveness for all his failings. The day after his death, I was saying the rosary in the garden, and I reflected that I had not had time to cry; I immediately burst into tears. And yet, in a monastery, we do not cry for the dead. That must not be seen as a lack of feeling on our part. We know where our brothers are going. The burials are always joyful. Our existence must be a novitiate for eternity. The entire liturgical life of a monk prepares him for the final hours. When the monks depart, I ask them not to forget us once they are in heaven. Sometimes, I tell myself that our brothers are so happy near God that they neglect us a little. We are in profound communion with our dead. We think of them every day."

In the tranquility of Solesmes, difficult deaths are all the more striking because they are rare: "The most horrible death was that of Father Guy Oury, November 12,

2000. He was the master of novices, and he collapsed in the refectory in front of the whole community. We were standing, I had begun to say the blessing. Our brother let out a horrifying, high-pitched cry, and he collapsed with all his weight to the floor. I rushed forward to give him absolution. God was already waiting for him; Father Guy fell into a deep coma, and he died a few moments later. The psychological blow was intense. We resumed the meal. But we were shattered."

Dom Philippe also told me about Brother Jean-Marie Lemonnier, who died of pancreatic cancer in 1999. He was a Breton, son of a farmer, a late vocation, and his endurance of suffering was incredible. He never complained. He was an example for the community with his unfailing patience when the cancer became aggressive. He spoke of his suffering only at the very end of his life. Five minutes before dying, he said to the father infirmarian: "It is the end. Yes, it is the end. I don't know how I am going to do it." He died gently. Dom Dupont had asked him to wait for his return from his trip before leaving earth. Brother Jean-Marie kept his word until the last minute of his life. This filial obedience *in articulo mortis* deeply touched the monks.

Without doubt, the "most beautiful death", to use Father Abbot's words, was that of Father Henri Rousselot, who left for heaven in 2013. He was ninety-six years old. His face in death was magnificent. He was supernaturally radiant. The monks had the impression that his features had been drawn by God. Everyone who entered his room was struck by this beauty. Each found the child that Father Henri had always been. This perfect death was far from being an exception: "At the moment of death of many of my brothers," Dom Dupont explained to me, "I knew that they were going directly to heaven. Brother Pierre was a saint. Father Rousselot and many monks died in the odor of sanctity. The old lay brothers have had difficult and bitter lives. But they retained a wonderful humility, constancy, and docility. While we were praying in the rooms of the dying, it has happened that we did not see them leave. The brothers were dead. The monks had seen nothing. I went forward to close their eyes. The monks often leave as they have lived. For most of them, the hour of death is easy, simple, clear. Some brothers have suffered. For them, God wanted a final purification. The monks who experienced cruel diseases nonetheless have a beautiful passing. At the last moment, their life is sweet."

Dom Philippe has a belief. In the last hours of our life, God prepares us for his arrival: "He wants us to be able to say 'yes' or 'no'. We sense him coming. We see a great light because God awaits our response. He asks us if we want him."

The Father Abbot had to leave. His heavy responsibilities were calling him away. My afternoon was also busy. I needed to meet the biological brother of Father Jean-Philippe, Father Joseph-Michel Lemaire. The principal infirmarian of the abbey since 1997, he told me humorously, "[I] was at that time perfectly incompetent. The sight of blood made me sick. When God gives a car, he also furnishes the fuel ... I learned everything on the job."

Among the monks whom Father Joseph-Michel accompanied in their final moments was Father Antoine des Mazis, who died of stomach cancer in 1975. "Father Antoine suffered greatly. We remember him as a scholarly, funny, absent-minded, and whimsical monk. At the end of his life, he lost his mind a bit. From his cell window, he was reliving the Second World War and tracking down

Germans. The last day, all the community came to say goodbye and embrace him. The monks were able to say a few words to him, to ask pardon, recall a memory. The final brotherly goodbyes are always deeply moving."

Several brothers have died in the arms of Father Joseph-Michel. In those moments, the hand is the last contact. It can reassure as never before. Father Guy Mesnard died in 2014. He had been one of the founders of the monastery of Keur Moussa, in Senegal. This frail monk was an ascetic and mystic. At the end of his life, he refused to eat. Father Guy was reassured when the infirmarians took his hand. He had a surprising interior strength, but he panicked when he sensed death approaching.

For Father Joseph-Michel, the monks "take care of the sick in the light of faith. We are a united family. From a material point of view, the work and the time we spend have no limits. We are caring for Christ himself. I was not prepared for this work. I had a vocation for work in education and childcare. Extremes are coming together."

In the beautiful guest garden where we were seated, Father Joseph-Michel discussed his personal limitations without reserve. One day a month, the infirmarian leaves to pray in an isolated chapel and take long walks in the forest. He loves to go to the sanctuary of Mont-ligeon. There, the nuns pray for him. He has the sense of accomplishing work that is complementary to that of his brother. Father Joseph-Michel is seventy years old, Father Jean-Philippe is seventy-nine: "I try to provide the best diagnosis, and Father Jean-Philippe reassures the patients by his mere presence. He is even-tempered and is remarkably gentle."

The infirmarians of Solesmes are lucky to have docile and joyful patients. There are not many who complain ... So Father Claude Gay, who died in 2003, was an exception: "This brother was a dissatisfied saint. A talented organist, a true artist, and extremely sensitive, he was depressive. You had to put him to bed one way, tuck him in another way, give him his medicine in a precise order that he alone established; the days were ritualized according to his anxieties. And yet, I am sure that God welcomed him to Paradise. In a monastery, the monks are preparing all their lives to meet God. Death is a violent rupture. The soul and the body are made to be together. If we live for ourselves, we are necessarily unhappy. If we live for Christ, we already have one foot in eternity. Some saints may have had bursts of fear at the last minute. The combat ceases only with the final heartbeat."

The bells were ringing. The father infirmarian said farewell to leave for Vespers.

The vigil of the feast of Pentecost, I left Solesmes. I carried with me the memory of Brother Pierre Buisson. In passing the cemetery one last time, I saw Brother Rémy. In overalls, he was explaining to a young retreatant how to prune roses bushes properly. His gravelly Mayenne farmer's voice was timeless.

One cannot leave behind the walls of Solesmes Abbey without a twinge of regret. With the monks, life is simple. However, it is possible to rediscover from some very distinguished pens the emotions and joys born on the banks of the Sarthe. Léon Bloy, Joris-Karl Huysmans, Simone Weil, Paul Claudel, Jacques Copeau, François Mauriac, Antoine de Saint-Exupéry, Pierre Reverdy, Paul Valéry, and Julien Green all loved Solesmes. In his *Petite suite bénédictine* (Little Benedictine suite), the journalist and poet Alphonse Mortier, a great friend of the monastery, composed some delicate verses that echo my personal experience:

I saw the cemetery where the Monks pursue
The ecstatic dream of their only Love.
They are scattered in the enclosure, and the nights
    and days,
Like an endless psalm whose responses follow each
    other,
In the brightness of days and fairness of nights.
The eternal liturgy, O Monks, for which you are,
And to the grave, pious interpreters!
Human memories, forever, have fled you.
Laid to rest in your robes, with their long,
    motionless folds,
Faithful to the Rule to the final verse,
Mystical servants of the humble Prophet,
Still you fulfill this difficult office....

On the lonely mound, I came to think.
June was shining with all its fire and the tall trees
Were gently shading the Abbey and its stones.
I was all alone, far away from the deceitful world.
The peace that you have known on our earth
And that you discover at the bottom of your graves,
Deep down, I was envying it, and you seem more
    beautiful
For having fulfilled with love your solitary lives.
And, under the bare turf, to enclose so much hope!
The hour was passing, clear as a bright sunrise
That never stopped giving its light....

And I would stay near you until evening,
When I heard the monastery bell ring
Calling to Choir your brothers, the living....

This fresh and pure morning, I often recall it,
O departed Monks. Benedictine shadows....

IV

The Smile of Brother Théophane

Sept-Fons Abbey

Near the gates of the Trappist abbey of Sept-Fons, little *In memoriam* cards are placed next to the prayer books. On the front, the photograph of a young brother, in a white habit, with a chubby face and beautiful dark eyes, serious and sad, looks into the distance toward a mysterious horizon. To accompany the image, the religious chose a simple message: "Brother Marie-Théophane, monk of the abbey of Notre-Dame de Sept-Fons, born December 7, 1961, first profession June 24, 1986, solemn profession

June 24, 1989, at rest in the peace of God on December 7, 1989, his twenty-eighth birthday, vigil of the feast of the Immaculate Conception. Rich in human and intellectual gifts, he completely fulfilled his monastic vocation in the righteousness of his heart after a long illness."

The short note ends with a moving prayer by Father Jérôme, a monk of Sept-Fons: "During my life you have held me by the hand, O my Mother. Could it be that at this hour I feel your fingers loosen and your hand let go of me? Certainly not! If your sovereign hand were leaving my hand, it would undoubtedly be to take a fold of your mantle and cover me with it. Mother of my long journey and Mother at my ultimate moment, yes, wrap me in the fall of your mantle during this short moment, after which, sure of having passed through the gate, I will suddenly let go, to make you hear my laughter. The laughter of a child, who laughs, who laughs, because, with the help of his Mother, he has achieved all."

Tucked away in the valleys of Bourbonnais Sologne, a small countryside of moors and wild ponds, not far from the city of Moulins, the abbey, which belongs to the Order of Cistercians of the Strict Observance, has not forgotten anything about the brief life of this young man who would not have had time to live. Sept-Fons is one of the most important abbeys in France. Eighty-five monks, often young, occupy these beautiful eighteenth-century buildings. The long white façades run around a series of large courtyards. Behind, the fields extend up to the banks of the Loire.

During our meeting, the Father Abbot, Dom Patrick Olive, remembered without difficulty the painful twists and turns of the brain tumor. In the month of December

1989, the Berlin wall had just fallen, history was advancing with giant steps, and Brother Théophane, unknown to all, was leaving the world, carried away by a final respiratory crisis.

When he died, the community felt like they were falling off a high cliff. How could it be imagined that the glioblastoma, as the doctors called this cancer, would end by having the last word? The power of faith did not prevent the rejection of death. The conviction of the monks was beautiful and bold. Dom Patrick did not want to doubt. God would answer his prayer. One day, however, he had to accept the facts. Brother Théophane was not being healed, his illness was getting irreversibly worse, and death was approaching. Dom Patrick said humbly: "I understood then that God's plans were not ours. He does not run the world as men imagine."

The young man from Lorrain entered the monastery in December 1983. He remained a monk for six years at Sept-Fons. It was in coming to visit his brother, who would become Brother Sébastien, that he discovered the place for the first time.

At the end of the intensely hot month of June 1986, he had two strange fainting spells. The Father Abbot asked Brother Samuel to accompany Brother Théophane to the Clermont-Ferrand hospital for an x-ray. The verdict was terrible. Brother Théophane had an aggressive cancer, a malicious poison that would soon destroy his most fundamental abilities. Today, as in the time of Brother Théophane, science is incapable of eliminating this evil.

The doctor thought his life expectancy would not exceed eighteen months. Dom Patrick was in the cloister when he learned the news. In shock, he almost lost his balance and fell to the ground.

At his return, Brother Théophane asked the Father Abbot if he was willing to keep him at the monastery. Dom Patrick did not hesitate for a second. The love and faith of the community were the two strongest crutches that allowed him to walk the designated path of death.

As long as the illness did not change the personality of Brother Théophane, he demonstrated unfailing will-power. But he had to get used to the daily life of the very sick, because the tumor was rapidly expanding its control. Whole days in bed, bedpans, violent headaches, the tyranny of ever-increasing medications punctuated his days.

From the beginning of his cancer, a facial paralysis disfigured him. Then, in October 1986, he began long and grueling radiation therapy at the Moulins hospital. Every day, a monk crossed the Allier countryside to drive him to the small radiology clinic. At the end of several weeks, coming back from a session, Brother Théophane passed his hand through his hair. A tuft of it remained in his fingers. The young patient was shocked but tried hard not to show it.

The radiation had an efficaciousness that surpassed all hopes. Between January 1987 and April 1989, Brother Théophane experienced a remission. He could resume his path. Dom Patrick believed that complete recovery was near.

One day, shortly before his death, Father Jérôme had said to the master of novices, Father Nicholas: "Brother Théophane is solid. Hold him fast, you will make of him a great monk!" The young Trappist was pure.

During the last months of his life, the monks often heard him reciting a poem of Verlaine that he knew in its entirety, "My Recurring Dream":

I often have a strange and searing dream
About an unknown woman whom I love
And who loves me. Never quite the same
Nor someone else, she loves, she understands me.

Yes, she understands; the pity is
For her alone my heart is obvious,
Simple for her alone who brings to life
My dead face running with her tears.

Is she dark, auburn, blond? I don't know.
Her name? It echoes
Soft as names of loved ones gone for good.[1]

By reciting these verses, he felt his memory was not slipping away from him. This was reassuring to him.

At the end of December 1988, Brother Théophane suddenly became anxious. But the medical tests were good, and no one was worried about it.

After the 1989 Easter holidays, the master of novices realized he had difficulties putting his thoughts down on paper. He became incapable of writing straight. His irrational fears were growing stronger and stronger. Dom Patrick asked the doctors to examine him again. The verdict of the scan showed no mercy. Brother Théophane was lost, the tumor had made rapid progress. Hope was becoming an illusion. He was a condemned man.

The monks did not give up. For eight months, they worked to try to save him, organized, hurried, attentive, hardworking bees, in an exhausting cycle.

Brother Théophane wanted to stay as long as possible in the *dormitorium*. He waited to be at the limits of exhaustion to move into the infirmary. His particular rhythm of life

[1] Paul Verlaine, "My Recurring Dream", in *Paul Verlaine: Selected Poems*, trans. Martin Sorrell (Oxford: Oxford University Press, 2009), 13.

could create difficulties for the other monks. Some were openly annoyed by it without fear of revealing unattractive selfishness.

On June 24, 1989, Brother Théophane pronounced the vows of his solemn profession. Less than six months before his death, he was singing solo, surrounded by the whole community, the traditional verse: "Receive me, Lord, according to your word and I shall live; do not disappoint me in my hope."

The fight against cancer, the progress toward death, did not undermine the monk's thirst for freedom. Quite the contrary, he went for a walk barefoot in the fields, lay down in the fresh grass, and dreamed of great voyages to the end of the world.

In *Qui cherchait Théophane* (Who was seeking Théophane),[2] the book that Father Samuel devoted to him, a passage describes the emotions and desires of a young man of his time: "He needs some relaxation, and we know he is a music lover. So, we give him a tape recorder and cassettes. To the great surprise of the purists, Brother Théophane reconnects with the singers of his youth: Joan Baez, Crosby, Stills, Nash & Young, and Simon and Garfunkel each share the infatuations and distastes of the patient in turn."

Ruthless, violent, the cancer wanted to win the game. The doctors were prescribing large doses of cortisone to fight against the edema that had formed in his brain. The face of Brother Théophane was deformed and bloated. The charming young man, slender, with poetic looks, became puffy.

---

[2] Père Samuel, *Qui cherchait Théophane* (Les Plans-sur-Bex: Paroles et silence, 1999).

One July afternoon, awaking from a nap, Brother Théophane did not recognize his room. Everything in the room was new to him. The color of the sheets, the icon hanging on the wall, the alarm clock on the nightstand were foreign to him. These symptoms marked the prelude to a major crisis. Brother Théophane was delirious, and the fever kept climbing. The monks took turns by his bedside trying to refresh his body, which had become so hot. Fortunately, the night was calmer, and the patient recovered little by little.

How could Brother Théophane not rebel against the injustice of his life, which had been torn to pieces? Despite the sufferings, the immense fears, he never complained. He confronted the cruelty of evil with the radicalism of faith.

In the final months, his personality had altered. The monks hardly recognized the enthusiastic, conscientious, and determined young man from Lorrain whom they had loved. He was losing his short-term memory. His sleeping was haphazard. For the brothers, the turns of keeping vigil in his room became a little way of the cross.

At the end of the summer of 1989, tests showed a pulmonary infection. Brother Théophane again set off for the Moulins hospital. The monks were not yet finished with traveling through the wise and deep countryside. In the evening, in the car that passed through the villages with the bucolic names they knew so well—Chevagnes, Garnat-sur-Engièvre, Dompierre-sur-Besbre—to return to Sept-Fons, the Trappists found a little peace in the heartbreaking beauty of the autumn lights that were falling into the fields and the undergrowth. The colors were in unison with the storms in their hearts.

Every week, Brother Théophane was a little more fragile. In this disjointed life, between the monastery and the hospital, he was losing his last points of reference. At the approach of All Saints' Day, the Father Abbot realized that Brother Théophane would not get better. He decided to bring him back for good. On November 11, 1989, after several epileptic seizures, he returned to his home.

The young monk had another trial in store. He became nearly blind. The monks quickly perceived it and respected this extraordinary humility. The patient was reaching the summit of a mountain after a hard climb. Soon the final bend was in view: Brother Théophane lost his speech.

From then on, the religious did not know precisely what his level of consciousness was. A painful infection required the infirmarians to bandage the eyes of the patient. Death was approaching. Brother Théophane was on the path to eternity like an outlaw who climbs the scaffold.

Breathing difficulties were leaving him like a dismantled puppet, the body broken, without breath. His eating was becoming problematic because he could not stop choking. On December 7, 1989, around seven in the evening, a stroke quickly carried him away. Outside, the church bells were ringing for Compline.

The final attack had deformed his face. Then, a few moments after death, in an instant, he recovered the beauty of his youth. Brother Théophane became again forever a young man with a fair, fierce, passionate complexion.

In his book, Father Samuel talks about some of the heart-breaking and luminous moments that followed the death of the monk:

> On December 9th, while I was praying near the body, in the silent church, at the time when the community is in the refectory, I heard a small footstep: a child, a very young boy from Brother Théophane's family, had

finished his meal and was approaching. After giving me a big smile, he unzipped his parka to take out his brother's wallet that we had just given him (the youngest, even more proud, had had the knife!). He took from an interior pocket a corded rosary that had the same origin, and, very devotedly, he knelt down. It was very moving to take in, in a single glance, the face of the young monk and that of the child, opposite him, who was praying. But little by little, emotion overcame the child; the tragedy of the scene outweighed the joys of the gift. Heavy silent tears were rolling down his face. Embarrassed, I changed places to draw closer to him. Happily, Brother Sébastien arrived. He picked up his brother under the arms, put him on his feet, heartily embraced him, shook off the sadness in a flash, and made a smile return in its place.

Twenty-eight years later, the Father Abbot remains convinced that the death of Brother Théophane reveals a divine teaching. For him, in carrying away a monk in the prime of life, God wants to show men that he is the only Lord of life and that men are not masters of their death. He has his reasons, and it is not given to us to understand them.

If the young Trappists of Sept-Fons were shocked by the death of their brother, through the sorrows and tears, they felt they were closer to God. "He comes to look for us like he went to pick up the lost sheep", explains Dom Patrick. "In the cemetery, we ask the Father to place us on his shoulders to carry us to heaven. We made the same request of him the day of our solemn profession. There is a thread that connects this commitment with the prayers of the final moments."

After the death, the infirmarians dressed the brother in his cowled robe and his scapular. They took him to the church, where he stayed two days. During those hours, the prayer of the monks never ceased.

At Sept-Fons, the rites surrounding death are recorded in the *Livre des us* (Book of customs). In the Cistercian tradition, from the death throes to the cemetery, the sick person who is leaving the world is never alone. The monks are present to ease his suffering. They guide him in his crossing to the other shore; they watch over him after his death, and they carry him into the earth.

The prayer of the dying is sweet and soothing. When the hour turns critical, the sacristans ring the bells in a special way so that the monks can quickly get to the infirmary. Sometimes a brother dies during the recitation of prayers, in the middle of the readings and the litanies.

Right after the death, the monks sing the *Subvenite*: "Come to his assistance, Saints of God. Hasten to meet him, Angels of the Lord. Receive his soul, offer it now in the sight of the Most High. Christ has called you. May he now welcome you, and may the Angels lead you to Abraham. Welcome his soul, offer it in the sight of the Most High. Lord, give him eternal rest; and may perpetual light shine upon him. Offer his soul in the sight of the Most High."

In a Trappist monastery, the deceased is buried without a coffin. The monks leave the cemetery when the body is covered with the earth that will be his last cloak while waiting for the resurrection. Before returning to the church, leaving behind them the body of their brother, the monks prostrate themselves, repeating the invocation three times: "Domine, miserere super peccatore." They stay a long moment with their heads bowed to the ground. The Trappists call this final gesture of prayer the "prostration on our knuckles". It comes from

Clunesian funeral traditions codified in the thirteenth century.

At the burial of Brother Théophane, the Father Abbot said this particularly evocative prayer: "Lord, it is great boldness for a mortal who is ashes and dust to recommend to you, our Lord and God, another mortal, ashes and dust. But, sure of your love, we implore you with faith: while the earth receives that which comes from the earth, welcome to the true homeland, near Abraham your friend, the one you have just taken from this world. Spare him from the fire of Gehenna, let him not suffer any harm, but, flooded with your joy, let him find rest in you. Let him not receive punishment for his faults, but let him taste the sweetness of your forgiveness. Let him rise again, a new creature, and join the host of saints who take their place at your right hand so as to receive the crown, when this world comes to an end, and let the light of the kingdom shine forth for all. We ask you this through Jesus Christ, our Lord." The last sentence of the Father Abbot, at the end of a long ceremony, resounded with a simple and joyful echo: "Let us go and keep before God the memory of our brother." In procession, the community then left the cemetery of Sept-Fons, which resembles a little forest dotted with worn and skeletal crosses.

When I came to see him in April 2017, Dom Patrick was going through an unusual experience. The community had lost five brothers in the space of a few months. The first one in this dark series died on November 10, 2016, and the last on April 2, 2017. With the precision and calm from which he never deviates, Dom Patrick spoke to me of these special times: "At the last burial, when I returned from the cemetery, I asked God to give us a little rest.

Since I became Father Abbot, I have never experienced such a storm. The community should accept this beautiful mystery. In 1997, we had buried a brother in the afternoon, then a second was dead the following morning. God often calls in groups."

During the course of his life at Sept-Fons, Dom Patrick was struck by the long and painful agony of one of the brothers. From the moment when the monks began to watch over the brother, they did not leave him for thirty-seven days. In fact, the Trappist tradition desires that a priest be at the side of the dying at all times.

In 1970, there were not enough religious at Sept-Fons to watch over the patient for so long a time. The young monks had to take part in the vigils. Dom Patrick was twenty-three years old. One week before the death, he was in the infirmary room. He was saying a rosary watching an elderly father who was not able to die. He was suffering a lot. His breath was short, and he groaned in pain. In those times, the infirmarians gave few painkillers. Dom Patrick was impressed: "I told myself that one day I would be in his position. I was already wondering if I would have his courage."

Since his abbatial election, Dom Patrick has seen forty-two monks die. All died in peace: "In the Gospels," he tells me, "the kingdom of heaven is promised to men who separate themselves from the riches and goods of the world. Saint Mark even states that we will have a hundredfold here on earth. How can we know what this hundredfold signifies? A good death is a part of the hundredfold. The prayer and the presence of the brothers help the dying monks a great deal. They make the final hours peaceful."

In the mid-1970s, Dom Patrick had the care of an old priest at the end of life. This monk was a colossus, with a strong personality and who freely expressed his thoughts.

He had entered Sept-Fons in 1909. When Dom Patrick was a novice, he had been his assistant as an electrician. He knew nothing about his new work, and he was often chastised. Dom Patrick wondered if he would be able to help him in this final trial. But the sickness had completely pacified him. He allowed himself to be led with a docility that the monks had never experienced in him.

Dom Patrick is a realist: "God does not spare monks from disease and suffering. We must go through these trials with a strength that is rooted in our faith. I cannot deny that medications have changed a lot. Pain is not treated in the same way. The process of dying is different. Evolution exists for better and for worse. At Sept-Fons, we want the brothers to die at the abbey. We try to be on good terms with the hospitals and the clinics so that they warn the father infirmarian when the time has come to bring back our own." He was thinking of Brother Jean-Lazare, who died in this fiftieth year, in December 2016. This monk was suffering from a devastating case of leukemia: "We diagnosed the disease in February, and he died ten months later. During the summer, he had a transplant. For him, this was a step toward getting better. We hoped, prayed, dreamed, but God wanted to reclaim him. The transplant turned against the body and set into motion a series of increasingly painful dysfunctions. After this operation, he was still staying at the Clermont-Ferrand hospital, in a sterile room, with a very strict protocol. Every day, we would visit him, which meant four hours of driving. I saw that his health was showing no sign of improvement. Brother Jean-Lazare did not really understand the reality of his condition. He loved life, and he believed in a remission. But he could see clearly that the treatments were not working. One morning, we learned of his father's death. He had been going through a difficult time for several months. I asked God to keep him alive until the departure of our brother: 'My God, if you are good, allow Brother Jean-Lazare to depart before his father.' We told his doctors that we did not want him to die in the hospital. How could we conceive of a brother leaving alone, surrounded by tubes, in an intensive care unit? The monastery doctor supported our request. I understood that the hospital staff wanted to keep him. They did not want to look like they were giving in; and they decided to send him back to the Moulins hospital, telling us they could do nothing more. His father died on the day of the transfer. After hesitating, we made the decision to tell him. From that moment on, Brother Jean-Lazare understood that his life was hanging by a thread. He accepted the deadline that was approaching. He died three days later. I had asked the Moulins hospital to stop treatment in order to bring him back to the monastery. They understood our request. Brother Jean-Lazare came back at noon on a Friday, and he died on Saturday at five in the evening."

Dom Patrick also spoke to me about the difficult hours they lived through with Brother Paul, who died at the age of eighty-two in March 2017. Pancreatic cancer carried him away in three months. When Brother Paul understood that the disease was irreversible, he fell into a depression. Then the monk accepted his fate, and he found peace again. Brother Paul was suffering enormously. The doctors began a morphine treatment. But the pain regained the upper hand. The hospital proposed going to a stronger treatment, warning the Father Abbot that there was a great risk that it would hasten the end: "I understood that this was a graceful way of telling us he was going to die as a result of his treatment. A doctor friend strongly advised us not to accept their proposal. He took responsibility for forbidding the chemical cocktail. I requested that Brother

Paul return to the abbey. As a result of his treatment, he was already in a slight coma. I have always had the feeling that the dying remain conscious until the end. They are separated from the living only by physical dysfunctions. I do not believe that a man can be totally cut off from the world. I have acquired this certainty after having accompanied so many monks to death. Brother Paul did not stay long in our infirmary. He died three days later. For the first time in my life, I had been confronted with a situation where painkillers could precipitate death. The line is blurred. Can I speak of disguised euthanasia? Without the help of a doctor, would I have understood the proposition that was made to me? The fight against pain can become a way of killing. Forty years ago, we were powerless in the face of pain; today, the problem is the opposite. For us, the most important thing will always be that the brothers are not alone when they depart. I know that our contemporaries often die in great solitude. Of the last five deaths, three brothers left before my eyes. We have been constantly at their side."

Every day at Sept-Fons, the brothers read the obituaries of the monks who have died at the abbey since the return from exile, in 1845. At the end of lunch, in the refectory, a monk reads them out loud.

Thus, on February 23, the eve of the anniversary of his death, the community honors the memory of Brother Marien Cluzet, a lay brother of Sept-Fons who died in 1904, whose death must have been striking: "Born in Artoire—Creuse—in 1819, entered Sept-Fons in 1854. He was the assistant guestmaster for a long time; he was revered by the guests and his brothers, being for all a model of charity and humility. He died a holy death on the feast of Saint Matthias. On his deathbed, he had been motionless and mute for three days when suddenly he sat up, lifted his eyes and arms smiling, then fell back, breathing his last. Mary, whom he had loved so much and served so well, had just introduced him to heaven. He was eighty-five years old."

Some departures are simpler, sometimes even marked by lightness. In 1971, Brother Gérard was dying. A lay brother with a very strong personality, the former sacristan of the Bourges cathedral, he had returned to Sept-Fons after several departures. He was in charge of the chicken coop. There, Brother Gérard took care of a famous cat, called Minette. At the approach of his death, Brother Alain, a very pious monk, was charged with accompanying him. He saw that Brother Gérard was in bad shape. He approached and asked him to repeat the invocation: "Jesus, Mary, Joseph, I give you my heart, my spirit, and my life." Brother Gérard did not respond. He then said to him: "Jesus, Mary, Joseph, assist me on my deathbed." He still was not responding. Brother Alain was not discouraged: "Jesus, Mary, Joseph, allow me to die in your holy company." Brother Gérard then cried out: "And what about Minette?"

The Father Abbot of Sept-Fons has accompanied so many brothers that he well knows the expression of men who will soon be leaving: "I am not afraid of being by their side. The face of a monk whose hours are numbered looks like a mask. At the moment when the soul leaves it, the body is transformed. Before death, the features are often tense, unpleasant; then they appear suddenly relaxed, at peace. We notice it all the more when the brother has suffered. The expression is fixed and does not move. Some of the dead are beautiful, and others a little less so."

When I asked him how God shows himself when a soul leaves the body, Dom Patrick responded as simply as if he were talking to me about an everyday occurrence: "I am never so much aware of the presence of God as at the moment of the death of my brothers. There is a break, a before and an after. We are at the point of the most perfect intersection between God and the living. I am not speaking about a feeling, a perceptible sensation, but of the certainty of faith. Death is the time of the realization of the promises of the faith. Suddenly, life stops. God comes and goes away with our brother. Without God, man is in an utter absurdity. If the end stops in a hole in the ground, life is not worth the trouble."

When a monk suffers too much, he cannot pray as before. In these moments, a mysterious alchemy is created; the patient is picked up by the flow of the prayers of the other monks. The man who is going to die can no longer row the boat, but he goes forward with his brothers. Others take the oars for him. Can God do without the prayer of the dying? Dom Patrick believes that if we can no longer pray, it is enough to be with God: "Before a monk is caught in the nets of sickness, prayer is the best attitude, the useful wisdom, the only necessity. The last thing that the dying lose is hearing. In a monastery, they hear up until the last second the prayers of their brothers."

Despair can overtake a dying monk. Suffering causes fatigue. Temperament plays an important role. Anxious brothers often have difficulties in overcoming these barriers. The Father Abbot must take the time to listen to the religious who are fighting against headwinds. Often, two or three words are enough to get things back on an even keel. The day when Brother Paul realized that his cancer would win, he was discouraged. Dom Patrick went up to see him in the infirmary; the patient was dejected, depressed, sunk in an armchair that seemed immense. Brother Paul began to speak. Just being listened to did him good.

Dom Patrick often thinks of the words of Pierre Cardinal Veuillot on his deathbed, after he had fought a long fight against painful leukemia: "We know how to say beautiful things about suffering. I myself spoke about it with warmth. Tell the priests to say nothing about it: we do not know what it is, and I have cried about it." In front of a man who is suffering, fine speeches are useless. They can only satisfy the healthy.

Brother Paul needed a discreet presence. He had never been one to vent his feelings. With disease comes a need to speak more, and Dom Patrick was there to listen to him. These warm little conversations were helping him to cross the ford. One night, the day before his death, the old monk said very quietly to the abbot, in his Alsacian wine-grower's accent: "You are my father, and I have no other father but you." Dom Patrick pressed his hand and remained close to him.

Man was not made for dying. Resistance in the face of this fated misfortune is always a striking thing.

In 1985, the winter of Father Jérôme was very painful. This great figure of the abbey marked a generation of monks who were nourished by his rigorous and prophetic instruction. For several months, the monks watched him fade away. The day before his death, he had a first heart attack. His breathing was painful. The monks put him on oxygen. But they did not want to take him to the hospital because they knew that the end was imminent. During the night, Father Jérôme was peaceful. Dom Patrick stayed the whole night at his bedside. In the early morning, he had another attack. The monks went to his room to pray. The bottle of oxygen could no longer ease his breathing. He died in a final choking fit. About twenty brothers were around him.

Gently, Dom Patrick told me: "Things happened as we had hoped. How could I envision Father Jérôme falling into a state of dependence? God spared him the humiliation of a bedridden state. His independent and free personality would have made it difficult for him to be reduced to the rank of an impotent old man. Despite the difficulties, his death was an accomplishment and a victory."

In 1968, Father Jérôme had written in his notebook: "Thanks to you, Lord, my life flows according to a remarkable continuity of trials and forced abandonments, without clearing, almost without clarity. Yet, beneath these troubles, you have all the same succeeded in helping me obtain the two or three goods that I imagined I would reach by daring and success and that arrived quite gently in silence and acceptance. We must dare to say: 'never mind' to all human abandonment, in order to be able to say to any divine offering: 'I take, I am a taker.' And you have led me, with the most perfect precision, exactly to the place, where, in my most gratuitous ambition, I wanted to go. Not toward sensual or spiritual delights, but to love for you, founded on truth and capable of lasting."

Tuesday, January 29, 1985; Thursday, December 7, 1989.

Father Jérôme, Brother Théophane. Two unique stories and two beautiful souls who have flown away.

V

Rainy Days

Cîteaux Abbey

On March 21, 1098, under the direction of Abbot Robert, twenty-one monks from Molesmes Abbey arrived at a secluded place. In the heart of the marshy forest of Cîteaux, they wanted to live together in a more authentic way, according to the rule of Saint Benedict. The early stages were difficult. The abbey was distancing itself from the Cluniac order's extravagance, but it attracted few novices.

In 1113, the hand of God seemed to come to the help of the reformer monks. Étienne Harding, third abbot of

Cîteaux, welcomed Bernard de Fontaine, who arrived
with some thirty companions wanting to be formed in
the monastic life. In 1115, Bernard in turn left to estab-
lish the abbey of Clairvaux. The charisma and tenacity of
this young man assured the order a rapid growth, and the
foundations multiplied. The Cistercian epic was beginning. It would not stop. In 1153, at the death of Saint
Bernard, the order of Cîteaux numbered three hundred
monasteries of men. By the end of the twelfth century,
there were five hundred ...

When coming to Cîteaux, how can one envision and
rediscover the traces of this past glory? On a rainy day in
May, I arrived from Dijon to spend a few days in the his-
toric abbey, after having crossed the lush, rich Burgundian
countryside. The metallic sky oscillated between gray,
black, and violet. Huge clouds were rolling toward the
forests of Nuits-Saint-Georges.

In passing through the beautiful gate that opened onto
a long drive, I was struck by the austerity, bareness, and
gravity of the place. The Cistercians have always cultivated
an ascetic detachment; it was normal for the radicality of
the place to affect my view.

The monastery is organized around an imposing
eighteenth-century building, the Lenoir wing, where the
ground floor gallery measures almost 110 yards long. In
the gardens, at the center of a perfectly mowed lawn, a
giant crucifix stands in front of the building. In the setting
sun, it casts its shadow on the white stone of the façade.
The monks' cells occupy the upper floors. Farther on, at
the edge of the park, an imposing statue of Saint Bernard
completes this intimidating setting. The contrast between
the white-water channels and the sunken paths that cut

through the undergrowth is striking, evoking a romantic English park.

The church has been completely renovated. Ever since 1998, the nave, the choir, and the aisles form a large, white, bare rectangle. To love this place requires a strong, inner fire.

Opposite, guestrooms occupy a large farmhouse built in the middle of the nineteenth century.

The evening of my arrival, the sky was a dazzling pale blue. After Compline, a distinctive silence reigned. It was pouring rain, and I felt there wasn't a living soul in these lands of Saint Bernard.

At Cîteaux, more than elsewhere, the presence of the dead is felt. On the other side of the Lenoir wing, the cemetery seemed immeasurable. A hundred graves were arranged around a beautiful stone cross. Unfortunately, the boxwood that decorated them was shriveling from the effects of a destructive parasite.

I went to Cîteaux to meet Father Olivier Quenardel. From the outset, I was struck by the strength, gentleness, and intelligence of his appearance. Born in 1946, he entered Cîteaux at the age of twenty. He was ordained a priest in 1988, then elected Father Abbot in 1993. Today, he is at the head of a community of twenty-six monks, four of whom live at Munkeby, a Norwegian foundation. Seven elderly brothers are in the infirmary.

Father Quenardel is a righteous and noble man who knows how to convince the person with whom he is speaking. Quiet, precise, and attentive, he might begin with an outburst of infectious laughter. As a young novice, he knew a different Cîteaux—where monks slept together in a *dormitorium*, where lay brothers could not be monks, where the Divine Office was in Latin. Since then, it has changed mostly to French, which, for some, was a bit of an ordeal, without, however, causing a crisis of faith.

At the beginning of our conversation, Dom Olivier wanted to tell me about the death of one of his predecessors, Dom Jean Chanut. Born in 1909, he entered the abbey at sixteen. At the other end of the road, in 1980, he died in Congo-Kinshasa, on the feast of the Assumption, after having prayed and sung all day with the African faithful. In the morning, he had celebrated Mass in the Mokoto monastery. Some hours later, accompanied by a villager whose family he had visited, he leaned his head on the shoulder of a young girl, who became a nun some years later. He told her: "It is a very great day today", and he died. Dom Olivier was moved as he told me about so discreet and beautiful a passing. His predecessor was a man of great faith. He should have died young. The novice master had told him one day when he was seriously ill: "My little child, this evening you will be with the good God." Dom Jean had seen the hour pass, and death had not come. At midnight, he was still there.

When they wrote a short history of his life, the monks wanted to highlight some of the amazing circumstances: "He crossed the threshold to eternity only after having been at the brink of death three times. He made his temporary profession in August 1928, and, in December, he was diagnosed with fairly advanced Pott's disease. He stayed in bed for two years and had a bone graft operation that was very successful, but, because of internal hemorrhaging, he was close to death and received Extreme Unction. From 1930 to 1938, he benefited from a little reprieve and spent those years in the effacement of communal life. It was then he would learn to become the beloved confidant of his brothers and a master of prayer. In 1938, his right kidney was lost and the left kidney was beginning to be affected by tuberculosis. He had an emergency operation, but the disease was winning. He would remain four years in complete rest in the infirmary from 1939 to 1943, each test finding traces of tuberculosis. At the initiative of a retreat master, a novena to Sister Elizabeth of the Trinity was made by the community, and, by the end of the novena, all trace of tuberculosis had disappeared. Eight days after the novena, he was riding a bicycle without any special fatigue. This recovery, totally inexplicable on a medical level, was recognized by the Church as a miracle obtained through the intercession of the one who would become Blessed Elizabeth of the Trinity. Father Jean came very close to death a third time following an operation, in 1968. He wrote in a statement, addressed to his whole community at the time of his resignation: 'These health problems have certainly been a source of great grace for me, and, far from complaining, I can in hindsight only humbly thank the Lord ...'; and, speaking of his abbatial office: 'In conscience, I believed I had to give myself completely, without thinking of my fatigue, believing that when God confers an important mission, he either gives the strength necessary to accomplish it or he removes the mission. Moreover, for me, relaxing my effort would have represented a collapse.' Familiar as he was with suffering and with death, it was through the participation in the sorrowful mysteries that he drew from prayer the grace of an ever more wonderful hope in the resurrection."

While continuing the account of the life of his predecessor, Dom Olivier wanted to tell me more about the unique relationship to death at Cîteaux. "In 1969, he resigned from his abbatial office. He was very tired, and he was truly depressed. Africa allowed him to rebuild himself. The holiest people can have large rough patches. One always imagines the monk in a sort of *apatheia*. In one sense, Épinal's image is not wrong. But one must never forget that monks get off track. Faith is like a little trickle of water that no longer manages to quench their thirst. Saint Thérèse of Lisieux had suicidal temptations. She even said that one should never leave medications within reach of the sick. The little Normand was up against a wall. She departed young, but she had an exceptional death. The Carmelite gave up her last breath pronouncing the name of Jesus, and the birds began to sing. In chapter 4 of his rule, 'The Tools for Good Works', Saint Benedict invites the monks to have death before their eyes every day. He goes on to ask them to keep a great desire for eternal life. For our founder, death and heavenly life are intimately connected. The Benedictine goal in death is eternity. Benedict of Nursia speaks of a longing for eternal life. This hope takes shape on the day of the funeral. The funerary liturgy of the monks is exceptional. We are joyful. The faithful are always struck by the peace that emerges from our ceremonies. The monks' bodies, with their faces uncovered in their cowled robes, are carried to the cemetery to the sound of hymns. By reciting Psalm 113, we symbolically express our departure from Egypt for the Promised Land. Sometimes families worry about these traditions, especially that the body of the monk is not placed in a coffin. For us, the corpse is a seed that goes down into the earth. It will bear fruit. Death is entirely enlightened by the mystery of faith. The families accompany us to the grave. After the burial, I always speak with the relatives of the deceased. I am struck to see how much people are affected. People are no longer sad because they understand that a life has just joined the Lord."

Dom Olivier found himself in the same situation at the death of his uncle, Brother Rémi. He was a monk at Cîteaux. Dom Olivier's parents had asked Brother Rémi to be the godfather of their son. Brother Rémi had refused because he already wanted to enter Cîteaux. Destiny wanted Dom Olivier to follow in his footsteps until his death: he died in 1986, the day of the fortieth birthday of his nephew. He was tired, and Brother Olivier had remained all morning in his room watching over him. Brother Rémi departed during the midday meal. At the end of lunch, the Father Abbot Loys Samson approached Brother Olivier and told him gently: "Brother Rémi has just died. It is your birthday present. You now have a godfather close to God."

Brother Rémi had received Extreme Unction, conferred on persons whose health raises serious concern. The Father Abbot has time and again observed the efficacy of this sacrament in the sick. It is a sacred act that can calm fears and give peace. Thus, at the beginning of 2017, the community gathered around Brother Hadrien in the oratory of the infirmary. He was ninety-five and walking with more and more difficulty. Brother Hadrien did not want a medically equipped cell. This old Cistercian was afraid of the infirmary, which he associated with suffering and death. He never went to see the sick. One morning, he fell out of his bed. Alone, he had to stay on the ground a long time. The monks feared that the problem would be repeated. When Brother Hadrien at last decided to go down to a medically equipped room, Dom Olivier suggested he receive the sacrament of the sick. He responded without difficulty: "As you wish, Father Abbot." Since then, he has been in his new situation. He did not take anything to his new room. Thanks to the radio system, he can listen to all the offices as well as the Chapter meetings and the reading in the refectory. The brother is not bored. He is alone with God.

According to Dom Olivier, Brother Hadrien has never known such peace of soul and mind.

A few years ago, Dom Olivier asked medical professors from the Dijon University Hospital to come speak to the monks about palliative care, life-prolonging interventions, and sedation. He has not yet been directly confronted with these problems. He knows, however, that communities have to face them.

Naturally, the monks of Cîteaux are convinced that they must accept that God can come to take them at any moment. If doctors asked to take a very old brother in critical condition to the hospital, it is highly likely they would refuse. The monks will always prefer that a religious be able to die in the abbey. Dom Olivier cited the example of Brother Félix. He did not want to go to the hospital anymore. In the ambulance that was taking him to Dijon, he considered that it was not the disease that would cause him to die, but the loads of medications he would be asked to take. He did not want additional care. He was eager to see God. The rule of the monks of Cîteaux is simple: one has to die someday.

At the end of the afternoon, we went to the large abbey cemetery. At the bend of an avenue in this solemn enclosure, Dom Olivier turned to me and said: "The hardest death is the little daily death, when we are perfectly healthy. In life, we go from one death to another; they prepare us for the ultimate end. Little deaths of the ego are the big deaths, and they allow for a good death. Why do some monks experience more difficult deaths than others? I cannot explain to you the reasons why God distributes our final trials so unequally. Perhaps monks carry for others humanity's fears and anxieties. One day, my father told me that he was not afraid of death. I told him that this was not a sign of holiness. Peaceful deaths are not necessarily the most holy. Good monks can experience anxieties when they embark for heaven. How did our brother Cistercians in Tibhirine die? We are almost certain they were beheaded. Who can know if they were afraid? Their spiritual battles must have been terrible. Satan is present up until the final moments. He does not ease his infernal grasp. Why does God allow the devil to act as he pleases? Lucifer loves to sow trouble and despair. He is a monster of pride. But God has the last word. Acedia is one of the great trials of monastic life. Prayer becomes burdensome, *lectio divina* is impossible, communal life no longer makes sense. All monks have walked these rugged paths. Perfect monastic roads do not exist. One day or another, there is a kind of point of exhaustion. It is the moment of outcry, and it is a decisive time: 'Lord, save me!' The example of the Carmelites of Compiègne standing on the scaffold singing is enlightening. A monk might die alone; he is already in the Communion of Saints."

Some hours later, I met Brother Philippe. He had been the infirmarian at Cîteaux for many years. Ascetic, mystical, serious, Brother Philippe resembled Saint Maximilian Kolbe. Quickly, I realized I was in the presence of a man of extraordinary strength and courage. Brother Philippe was fifty, and he was already a master.

He himself lived through significant physical trials. One day, he went to find his abbot: "Father Oliver," he said to him, "I feel like a have a growth in my head." The tests revealed a benign tumor situated between the brain and the cerebral cortex. Brother Philippe continued his work up until his departure for the hospital.

After the operation for this acoustic neuroma, immobilized for a week in a hospital bed, he was overcome by violent headaches: "My trial was sent by God so I could grow in love and trust. All life is a school. I knew I was going to get through another stage of my life without knowing the content."

Should the monks reflect on death or on the way to live their death? For Brother Philippe, they have first and foremost a passionate and beautiful obligation to love life. I realized that he had learned not to be too afraid of suffering. For him, monks fall asleep in the Lord: "This morning, at four o'clock, we discovered a brother whose varicose veins in his leg had opened. He went into the hall to find me but I had left to open the church. He had placed a little towel around his leg waiting for my return. I had to walk in the blood to reach his bed. The brother was smiling, but he was becoming increasingly pale. I stopped the bleeding; then he was immediately hospitalized. Brother Henri realized he could depart at any moment. He was peaceful. At the end of their lives, men are not much anymore. The worn and withered shells of their bodies have value only for God."

The beginning of our conversation was difficult. Brother Philippe was strangely calm telling me about this elderly monk. I asked him to describe his daily life for me: "I have been at Cîteaux for twenty-five years. I made my solemn profession in 1998, and I have been a priest since 2009. In 1998, the Father Abbot asked me to be responsible for the infirmary. Before entering the monastery, I had never had contact with a sick person. Death was an unknown. I was completely dedicated to my task for ten years. This experience deeply affected me. I accompanied and buried twelve brothers. At the funeral, we dig a hole, about two yards deep. Surrounded by the community, the deceased brothers are lowered into the earth in the arms of the brother infirmarian, who lays them on a simple board. I am charged with standing in the grave to guide the descent of the body. So, I am the last to see the departed, before placing a white veil on his face." It is an important moment for the monks. In this life, they will never again see the brother whom they have known for so many years.

The great crossing over is the culmination of all monastic life, Brother Philippe insisted on this point: "Death is the moment for which we are waiting. We will die as we have lived. There are also exceptional situations. I accompanied three brothers who proved to be saints at the moment of death."

Brother Philippe was happy and emotional telling me about the departed monks who mattered in his life. As his story progressed, it seemed to me like a litany of ordinary and sublime deaths.

In 2005, Brother Marie-Joseph died at eighty-seven years of age. Diabetic and insulin-dependent, he died from repeated internal hemorrhaging. He bore the disease without showing anything of his suffering. One day he chose not to take any more pain medication: "I often made time to speak with him. I was trying to understand the exact depth of his suffering. The responses were always the same: 'The body is dead, but the spirit is living.' He often quoted Saint Paul in the Letter to the Philippians (3:21): '[Jesus will come again] who will change our lowly body to be like his glorious body.'"

The crudeness of Brother Philippe's words might shock. He did not want to hide anything about the hell of physical suffering: "By chance, I discovered that Brother Marie-Joseph was hemorrhaging. While washing him, I thought he was suffering from incontinence, but the rush of blood showed me the problem was more serious. I saw that his days were numbered. We could do nothing more than clean up his blood, which escaped at regular intervals."

Medical care was perfectly organized at the abbey. The old monk had no remaining family. Brother Philippe was amazed by his faith. The more he suffered, the more he prayed to the Virgin. Brother Marie-Joseph was of Basque origin. Before, in the *lavatorium*, the Cistercians would hear him singing Marian hymns in his native language. One day, when he was alone in his room, Brother Philippe said to him: "So, Brother Marie-Joseph, are you going to heaven?" The response, spoken in a hoarse voice, was wonderful: "Yes, and it will be a celebration like no other." Brother Marie-Joseph was at the point of death, and he was joyful. Three days before his death, he again confided to Brother Philippe: "I tried to live the Gospel."

The moment of his death was difficult. The community had gathered in the room. The assistant brother infirmarian urgently called Brother Philippe to warn him that the hemorrhaging was increasing in intensity. The monks left the room. When Brother Philippe arrived, he realized there was nothing he could do. The final attack was brutal: "There was a rush of blood, and we began to pray to the Virgin Mary. Overwhelmed by suffering, his eyes red, Brother Marie-Joseph was trying to say his prayers. His features were twisted by the pain. I did not think that at this point a face could be so transformed by convulsions. He was lost in prayer and suffering. I was struck by his faith, his courage, his integrity. I felt very small."

In an abbey, death is not always surrounded by this sense of spiritual grandeur. Brother Philippe insisted on this point: there are no rules in death. However, the end of a monastic life is always a moment of truth. At the approach of the fateful hour, barriers fall. Psychological knots, anxieties, and fears unravel. The brother infirmarian must take it upon himself to accompany this maieutic ending as best he can.

Brother Philippe has always known how to adapt to the different temperaments of the monks. His account of the last days of Father François-Xavier illustrates this in every respect.

Obedient, faithful, gentle, Brother François-Xavier was a Cistercian to his core. At ninety-five, he had retained the energy his youth. He smiled for no reason. Brother François-Xavier never saw the bad. But in the last months, the peace and serenity that had inhabited his heart were lacking. The monk felt he had missed the point of his life. He even thought that we would ask him to leave the monastery. When he returned from a stay in the hospital, he packed his suitcase. The Father Abbot asked him the reason for such a surprising action. He responded: "I must leave. After what I have done . . ." He never wanted to confide the nature of his supposed, reprehensible act. Another day, he went to see Dom Olivier, and he told him: "I'm no longer good for anything. I come to place myself in your hands." Brother François-Xavier imagined he had become a useless burden for Cîteaux. The monks had never seen him distressed. At the end of his life, he seemed to have experienced a great spiritual battle. Brother Philippe believes that "God clearly asked for a final purification from him. Our Father Abbot likes to remember that Christ himself did not die in tranquility. On the contrary, the Lord died in agony. One evening, I was in his room, and I saw he was agitated. Brother François-Xavier pointed with his finger to some sort of presence behind me. He was terrified by this thing. He could not define what he saw. I prayed my rosary by his side. After our prayers, everything had disappeared. I never understood the origin of his torment. What was the role of psychological delirium in Brother François-Xavier's troubles? How can we know if he was suffering from a hallucination or an attack of the Evil One? A few days later, he died in peace; he had regained calm and serenity when he breathed his last breath."

The day when a brother departs, the monks have the custom of getting together to exchange memories of the deceased. The moments that come to the minds of the monks are often beautiful, moving, and luminous.

The story of Brother Marie, the younger brother of Brother François-Xavier, is striking. He was born into the Colas des Francs family. Brother Marie's character was simple, candid, and very kind. The monks loved him dearly. He had difficulty suffering. Consequently, he had the curious idea of reading a medical treatise by Saint Hildegarde von Bingen, the twelfth-century Rhineland mystic. His interpretations of the Benedictine nun's texts were sometimes bizarre. For example, he declared that he had to eat handfuls of raw nettles to stay healthy.

The monk had an extraordinary sense of service to the community. Even when he was completely exhausted, he rushed to open the doors of the church for the religious in wheelchairs. He loved his brothers with a pure love. Eight days before his death, the Father Abbot left Cîteaux to go visit the Norwegian foundation. Since Brother Marie was very tired, Dom Olivier told him: "For the love of heaven, do not depart for God until the end of my trip." The Brother knew the exact day of his return. At the very moment when Dom Olivier passed through the beautiful abbey gate, Brother Marie gave up his last breath. The monks were greatly impressed. Brother Marie was leaving as he had lived. Without noise, without affectation, without sorrow.

Among the sick whom Brother Philippe cared for, Brother Jean-Marie occupies a special place. He wanted to be like Thérèse of Lisieux, who said: "I do not die, I enter into life." However, like the little saint of Lisieux, he felt abandoned by God. At eighty, he was diabetic and bedridden. At the approach of death, he was lost in anxieties and endless obsessions. His life as a monk, however, had been joyful and peaceful.

In the infirmary room, he spoke to Brother Philippe about his suicidal thoughts. Dom Olivier did not understand the darkness of these impulses so foreign to Brother Jean-Marie's temperament. The monk spoke easily enough about his torments, but no one succeeded in helping him. He could become aggressive. Brother Philippe was worried, but remained convinced he would never take action.

His despair caused a stomach ulcer that worried the doctors. Completely worn out, he fell into a coma that lasted a week. He continued to show signs of distress and agitation. With the help of a psychiatrist friend, Brother Philippe tried to soothe him. At the suggestion of the community's doctor, he was given injectable Tranxene as well as some strong painkillers. It was not possible to obtain the consent of the brother, who could no longer communicate.

At the end of seven days, the monk opened his eyes, and, without seeing the infirmarian, then alone with him in the room, he exclaimed: "My Lord, my God and my All ...", then he fell back to sleep. The following day, his ulcer burst. "There was a spurt of blood, from his mouth, a yard and a half long. I was not prepared for such violence.

The brother who should have helped me did not respond to the bell I was desperately ringing to call for help. Without faith, I would not have been able to hold on. Praying intensely, and holding his head, I took a towel to mop up the blood."

Before falling asleep forever, Brother Jean-Marie and Brother Marie knew great suffering. But at the moment of death, their eyes were illuminated in an exceptional way. They were transfigured. Brother Philippe had never seen such transparent eyes. "There are no words to describe the purity that inhabited them. They had gone through the roads of purification through suffering. God was already with them. In a flash, the hardship of pain had given way to the infinity of joy. I can still see the light of their eyes. I will never be able to forget that sublime color which was no longer human."

Brother Philippe experienced equally difficult crises and similarly divine wonders with Brother Laurent. Aggressive leukemia carried him away. He died one month after receiving the diagnosis. His life was nothing but a bed of pain. During those few weeks, he never complained. Every day, Brother Philippe had to replace his bandages: "His legs, and especially his calves, rapidly turned into necrotic sores. Every day, I had to spend a short hour at his feet, while he was seated in the chair, undoing, as gently as possible, the bandages of the previous day, which stuck to the sores, despite all precautions, and applying new ones to him. The leukemia prevented the regeneration of his skin, and the open sores spread over the entire surface. I knew I could not cure Brother Laurent, but only give him some relief. This feeling of impotence was difficult. The doctor and the dermatologist could not stop the work of the necrosis."

Brother Laurent spoke little. When Brother Philippe changed the bandages, he learned to communicate with him through facial expressions and signs. Gentleness was still possible. One night, before going to sleep, the old monk calmly told a novice: "In my youth, I very much wanted to follow Jesus on the Cross; I talked a lot about it; and now I am there, and I am silent."

Brother Philippe had to arm himself with courage: "One morning, I discovered that Brother Laurent had taken off all his bandages, and the naked sores had bled onto the sheets. I left for a short moment to pray to regain my calm. Brother Laurent, like all Cistercians, was used to solitude. By this action, he was demonstrating a kind of revolt against the barbarism of this last stage of his life."

However, Brother Laurent showed no bitterness. In suffering, he was peaceful. One morning, as usual, Brother Philippe helped him to get dressed. All of a sudden, he collapsed and gave up his spirit. Brother Laurent fell like an angel deprived of his fragile wings. He was smiling.

Rapid deaths are often even more impressive than painful deaths. Father Tarcisius was a generous monk. For several years, he had been afflicted with Parkinson's disease. He collapsed in a hallway. The religious placed him in a wheelchair to rush him to the infirmary. He died in this wheelchair. The paramedics tried to resuscitate him. But he was already with God.

Every day, the monks try to think of their dead. Why reflect on the last things just at the moment of departure? It is rather unreasonable to think we are going to meditate on death when we are sick and tired.

Brother Jérôme had the symptoms of Alzheimer's disease. He knew he should prepare himself for death before his memory left him. He died in his sleep.

I was struck to the heart by the strength, the generosity, and the simplicity of Brother Philippe.

Before we parted, I asked him if he wanted to add anything. I can still hear the sound of his deep and meditative voice: "Thinking about death is not morbid. On the contrary, it enables us to understand the meaning of life. It is necessary to learn to recognize the end of our road. Why be afraid? The Resurrection is the foundation of our faith. Real life is not on earth. Every day, we must prepare to die."

No one can know how he will live his death. Will we be courageous, fearful, happy? Will we be cowards or heroes? If he had to depart under the same conditions as Father Jacques Hamel, assassinated during Mass at Saint-Étienne-du-Rouvray, Brother Philippe is unable to say if he would be as noble. He was struck by the final words of the priest: "Depart, Satan!" At the hour of death, our perceptions are not as acute. Life plays out in a fraction of a second. Brother Philippe loves the words of Christ in the Gospel of Saint Matthew (10:19): "When they deliver you up, do not be anxious about how you are to speak or what you are to say; for what you are to say will be given to you in that hour."

How would the brother infirmarian of Cîteaux like to be accompanied at the hour of his own death? He has no doubt that the brothers he has cared for, the sons of Saint Bernard who have suffered, the monks who died in his arms, will come to find him to reassure him.

"How can I still be useful to others?" How many times has Brother Philippe heard these words from the mouths of religious who have reached the threshold of the great voyage? The question seems surprising for a man at the end of his road. The brothers have worked all their lives, and they want to serve while drawing on the last of their strength.

At Cîteaux, there is a workshop for the old monks. They make rosaries that are sent all over the world. Three days before departing, a ninety-seven-year-old brother was working with just one hand; the other was paralyzed. He succeeded in finishing one last rosary.

As we were about to part, on the doorstep, Brother Philippe bid me farewell with one last story: "One day, a diabetic brother had passed a sleepless night. But he was radiant. With his usual enthusiasm, he explained to me that he had spent his time traveling the world sowing 'Hail Marys'. He told me that he had gone in spirit to all the continents, right to the end of the world. The brother had traveled the oceans before taking his vows. He was a sailor. The following day, he left us to sail on the waves of the good God."

Brother Philippe headed back to the infirmary, walking peacefully under the rain that was flooding the countryside.

I looked far away at the statue of Saint Bernard. He knew doubts and sorrows that are not far from those of the monks in our times. The great Cistercian mourned the death of his brother Gérard, who had been the cellarer of Clairvaux. In his twenty-sixth sermon on the Song of Songs, he spoke of his sadness in extraordinary detail:

> You understand how faithful a companion has been taken from my side "in the way in which I was walking." You know what was his attentiveness to duty, his diligence at work, his sweetness and amiability of character. Who was so indispensable to me? By whom was I so much beloved? He was my brother by blood, but more my brother by religious profession. Oh, pity my lot, you to whom these things are known!

I was weak in body, and he supported me. I was pusillanimous, and he encouraged me. I was slothful and negligent, and he spurred me on. I was improvident and forgetful, and he acted as my monitor. Oh, whither hast thou been taken from me? Why hast thou been torn from my arms, "a man of one mind," "a man according to my heart"? We have loved each other in life, how then is it that we are separated in death? O most cruel divorce, which only death could have power to cause! For when in life wouldst thou have so deserted me? Yes, it is unmistakably the work of death, this most woeful separation. For what but death, that enemy of all things sweet, would not have spared the sweet bond of our mutual love? With good reason is that called death and a double death, which in its rage has slain two in carrying off one. Has not that separation been death to me also? Yea, and especially to me, for whom is preserved a life more bitter than any death. For I live indeed, but only to endure a living death. And I shall call such an existence life? O unfeeling death, how much kinder it had been to deprive me of the possession of life than of its fruit! For life without fruit is worse than death, since we are told that two evils, the axe and the fire, await the tree that bears no fruit. Therefore, through envy of my labours, "thou hast removed far from me my friend and my neighbour," to whose zeal was mainly due whatever fruit those labours yielded.

Hence it were far better for me to have lost my life than thy company, O my brother, who wert the earnest stimulator of my studies in the Lord, my faithful helper, and my prudent counsellor. Why, I ask, have we been so united in brotherly love? Or, so united, why so parted? O most mournful lot! But it is my fate that is pitiable, not his. For thou, sweet brother, if separated from thy dear ones, art now united to others still more dear. But what consolation remains now to wretched me, after losing thee, my only comfort? Our bodily companionship was a source of enjoyment to both of us, on account of the conformity of our wills and sentiments, but I alone have suffered from our separation. The enjoyment was common, but I am left the monopoly of the sadness and the sorrow. "Wrath hath come upon me"; "wrath is strong over me." Sweet was the presence of each to other, sweet our companionship, sweet our conversation. But whilst I have lost the happiness of us both, thou hast only exchanged it for better. For in this exchange "there is a great reward."[1]

Reading these lines, I think of Brother Philippe. He has accompanied so many monks to the gates of eternity. Over the years spent with the sick in the infirmary, has he also lost all the joys described by Bernard of Clairvaux? The founder of the Cistercian order speaks of a "great reward". It is enough to observe Brother Philippe for a moment to know that they are innumerable and that they illuminate his life.

---

[1] Saint Bernard of Clairvaux, *Sermons on the Canticle of Canticles*, vol. 1, trans. A Priest of Mount Melleray (Dublin: Browne & Nolan, 1920), 285–86, https://archive.org/stream/stbernardssermon01bern.

VI

The Art of a Happy Death

Fontgombault Abbey

Fontgombault Abbey is nestled in the heart of the countryside. On the banks of the Creuse, on the Berry frontier, fields, forests, and caves surround the walls of the enclosure. The boscage protects Fontgombault from intrusive eyes.

Past the heavy wooden door of the porch, the abbey church reveals its splendor. At every office, a splendid group of Benedictines in black, entering the choir, impresses the pilgrims.

The Father Abbot Dom Jean Pateau and Dom Antoine Forgeot, his predecessor, lead the slow and solemn procession.

The Gregorian chant at Fontgombault is one of the most beautiful in the world. On Sundays, when the choir organ discreetly accompanies the monks, for solemn Mass or Vespers, the beauty of the voices reaches the sublime. The gentleness, precision, and richness of this music can transform a man.

In the church, at the height of summer, coolness caresses the skin. But in winter, the icy, wet, merciless cold can grip the body to the bone. On late-autumn nights, at the hour of Matins, the temperature rarely exceeds 40 or 45 degrees in the beautiful wooden stalls.

On this Wednesday in May, heavy rain was falling in gusts on Fontgombault. From the windows in the cell where the father guestmaster had placed me, I saw soaking-wet brothers passing through the courtyard. With their heads bent forward, they did not linger on the muddy road that led to the portal of honor.

In the evening, in the medieval refectory, the steaming soup finally warmed the monks. Streams of light were coming in through the high windows. From his pulpit, in the silence punctuated by the sound of utensils and dishes, the lector was reading through speeches delivered during a papal trip.

Then the melancholy of Compline again calmed hearts and souls. After the blessing, the monks came to kneel before the statue of Our Lady of a Happy Death. A few moments after my arrival, I had already seen Dom Antoine Forgeot praying before this Virgin. The flames from the candles illuminated the walls and pavement. His fingers slipped over the beads of a large rosary made of Job's

Tears. I could hear the murmurings of his voice. If one day I learn of his death, this image will come to mind. And I know I will weep.

At night, I could hear the far-off sound of water pounding in the reservoirs of a dam. Built along the Creuse, it allowed the monks to produce their own electricity. After the rain, a thick fog covered the countryside and abbey grounds.

Around seven in the morning, I went down to the abbey church. About fifteen monks were saying their daily Mass. In front of the small stone altars positioned near pillars facing east, they were offering their prayers for the world. I heard the murmuring of sacred words spoken in low voices.

A few prayerful faithful, some words in Latin, some attentive lay brothers, monks walking slowly, the hoods of their habits raised over their heads, a nave flooded with springtime light—this May morning, the grace of Font-gombault was ageless.

I went into the ambulatory of the church to see the tombstones of two former Father Abbots, Dom Roy and Dom Roux. They were on either side of the Blessed Sacrament altar. One day, Dom Forgeot and Dom Pateau will join them. Their places are ready.

In the little cemetery nestled right against the church, solemn white crosses stood out in the lush grass. At the back, a small white gate opened onto a magnificent apple, pear, and quince orchard. In the middle of the nineteenth century, the Trappists were in charge of Fontgombault. They were forced to leave it in 1903. Today, when the Benedictines dig new graves, they often find remains of the bodies and habits of their predecessors.

The great monastic chain spans the centuries. Émile Verhaeren, in his poem "To the Monks", describes this beautiful mystery:

Monks approaching us from gothic horizons,
whose soul, whose spirit of tomorrow dies,
who confine love to your mystic gardens
to purify it of all human pride,
resolute, you advance down the roads of men,
eyes deluded by the fires of perdition
from distant times to our present day,
through ages of silver and centuries of iron,
and ever the same step pious and broad.
Alone, majestic, you survive a dead Christian
   world
Alone with back unbowed you bear its load
like a royal corpse sunk in a coffin of gold.
Monks—seekers of sublime chimeras
your cries of eternity penetrate the necropolis,
your spirit is haunted by the glow of summits,
you are the bearers of cross and flame
around the divine ideal buried in the earth.

O monks, vanquished, unbowed, silenced,
O giants who tower above the din of the world,
who hear the only sound that heaven forged;
monks grown tall in exile and enslavement,
monks hunted down, but whose ruby garments
illumine the world's night, and whose heads
fade in the lucidity of supreme suns,
we, the peaceful poets, we magnify your forms.
And whilst no pride today is victor,
and palm leaves are trodden into the muck,
monks, great solitaries of thought and heart
before the last soul becomes extinct,
my verses will build you mystic altars
beneath the wandering veil of a chaste cloud,
that one day this soul in eternal desire,
pensive, lonely, despairing, in the depths of pale
   night,
will rekindle the fire of your extinguished glory,

will dream of you still when the final blasphemy
like an immense sword skewers God.[1]

Today, two figures represent Fontgombault Abbey. The
first is Dom Jean Pateau. He entered the abbey in 1990 and
was elected Father Abbot twenty-one years later. Calm,
smiling, intelligent, he always seemed to me the embodi-
ment of a righteous man. His abbatial motto sums up his
spirituality: "Modo geniti infantes" (Like newborn infants).

He wanted to explain this choice to his brothers. In a
moving text, he described his vision of the monastic ideal:
"Becoming a child implies a change, an effort, real work.
This transformation, however, is the indispensable condition for entering into the family of God, into his sanctuary,
into the kingdom of heaven, for entering into this game
that is the monastic life. But spiritual childhood, of what
does it consist? In a word, it is made of simplicity, trust,
complete abandonment in the hands of God.... Thus, the
monastic life is a life made for children. The monastic life
is a game, the great game of charity. In a game, it is necessary to respect the rules; it is the same in the monastic
life. The monastic life is a game played with God and with
those the Lord has chosen to lead to the monastery, those
we call our brothers. Truly, monastic life is a conspiracy
of charity."

In the rule, Saint Benedict calls on his sons to fear the day
of judgment, to be afraid of hell, and to desire eternal life.

Paraphrasing Ignatius of Antioch, Dom Jean Pateau
explained to me on several occasions that it was better to
die well than to reign over the ends of the earth: "Here
below, monks want to become transitory pilgrims."

[1] "To the Monks", in *Poems—Emile Verhaeren*, trans. Will Stone (Todmor-
den, U.K.: Arc Publications, 2013), 40, Google Play edition.

The second name associated with Fontgombault is that of Dom Forgeot. Born in 1933 in the Basque country, he chose to join the abbey at twenty, far from his homeland. His biological brother, Xavier, had already entered religious life. Then, from 1977 to 2011, he was the Father Abbot of the monastery.

He told me with simplicity about his arrival in Berry. Listening to him, I felt that monastic life was consistently happy. Dom Forgeot is aware of being the memory of the abbey. But he never dwells on the feelings of admiration that can be evoked by the sixty-five years he has spent at Fontgombault. Humble, wise, Dom Forgeot is a perfect image of an elderly monk at the end of his life. Slightly stooped, with a quick step and an alert intelligence, he has a keen view of the world. The former Father Abbot does not look for the right words; he describes things precisely and seriously.

Dom Forgeot has seen twenty-six monks from the abbey leave this world. But he does not have a single memory of a tragic or painful death. He remembers silent passings, in peace. Gentle deaths.

The death of Brother Clément touched him deeply. A lay brother, self-effacing and courageous, he spent his religious life in the abbey kitchens. Afflicted with Parkinson's disease, he lived in the monastery infirmary. One morning, he felt mildly fatigued. The father infirmarian advised him to stay in bed and get some rest. He saw that his condition was rapidly deteriorating. Dom Forgeot was quick to come visit him. When he entered his room, Brother Clément's breathing had greatly weakened. He gave up his soul without difficulty.

Dom Forgeot, who was still prior of Fontgombault, remembers with emotion old Father Julien. The Father Abbot Roy often told him: "You will not die in my absence." One winter morning, after a bad case of the flu, the doctor realized that the end was very near. But Dom Jean Roy was absent for the day. Dom Forgeot called him to tell him the bleak diagnosis. Dom Roy asked him to administer the last rites immediately. After dinner, Father Julien asked Dom Forgeot if the Father Abbot had returned. Dom Forgeot replied in the negative. He was breathing with infinite difficulty, but he was holding on. Two long hours later, Dom Roy returned to the abbey. He went to see him without delay, and Father Julien died in his presence. For Dom Forgeot, "he died in obedience."

In the Benedictine tradition, the Father Abbot is Christ's representative. The departing monks like to die in his presence.

In November 1956, Dom Forgeot was present at the death of his biological brother, Xavier. He died in Val-de-Grâce hospital in Paris. He was doing his military service. A stroke victim, he had little glimmers of consciousness, but he could no longer express himself. For two months, Brother Xavier Forgeot remained in this difficult state.

The two brothers had entered Fontgombault one year apart. Dom Forgeot has forgotten nothing about that winter night. At the moment of death, he was at his bedside with the Father Abbot Édouard Roux: "He died in peace. I was twenty-three years old, and my brother was twenty-five. We were prepared. At the time, there was no possible cure. For monks, death is formidable, like a punishment, but it does not frighten us. It is natural. Hope is everything. We are confident that death will not separate the people who have loved each other on this earth." Dom Forgeot told me about this sad event in his life with great modesty. A few months before, he had already lost his father, aged forty-nine years old.

The year 1956 was terrible. Dom Forgeot watched young Brother Philippe Vilain die. The two men had entered the abbey together and made their professions the same day. Brother Xavier and Brother Philippe died within six months of each other. At the time of his death, in a military hospital, Brother Philippe had a moment of fear. But Dom Forgeot and Dom Roux could not be at his side. The young shoots of Fontgombault were departing like summer grain fallen to the ground during a stormy night.

At the approach of death, within a monastery, problems subside and are simplified. Complicated, impetuous, our individualist monks become serene. Dom Forgeot always thought that we should pay attention to these signs because they announce the end: "It is very beautiful to see a monk who is aging well. God is faithful and helps us, on the condition that we allow it."

Is there a special grace at Fontgombault? In 1948, Dom Édouard Roux arrived from Solesmes with twenty-four monks. The great majority of the brothers were his former novices. The community had always been brotherly. They took possession of a monastery that had long been consecrated to the Blessed Virgin: "Mary protects us", Dom Forgeot told me. "She watches over the tranquility of the monastery with special care. In civilian life, the religious had the opportunity to choose his friends. But, inside an abbey, his brothers are given to him by God. Yet, in seventy years, the unity of Fontgombault has never failed. This peace is not unrelated to the joy of the monks at the moment of their death. It is important to say that our house possesses a statue of the Mother of God called Our Lady of a Happy Death."

The twelfth-century, limestone Virgin, over three feet tall, is represented in majesty, holding the divine Infant on her knees, just as the Romanesque sculptors liked to depict her. Her story is remarkable. In the middle of the eighteenth century, the monks had already left the place, victims of the complex benefice system. Sold to the Revolution as national property, the church was transformed into a stone quarry. A sacrilegious hand, that of George Sand, inscribed this graffiti on columns of the shrine: "Numquam Deo!" (May it never again be God's!)

At that time, an unfortunate man decided to attack the venerable statue to bring it down. Evil befell him: he took a serious fall, from which he died shortly after, repenting. From that day, the Virgin was henceforth invoked under the title of Our Lady of a Happy Death.

Today, the monks come every day to pray at her feet for the dying and hospitalized.

Dom Forgeot does not question the dedication of doctors. According to him, however, the latest medical advances risk leading to the theft of death. The excess of painkillers plunges the sick into nebulous states that cut them off from the moment they are going to experience: "It becomes dreadful to go to the hospital. Must one recover at all costs? The response of the monks is simple: men of God do not want to hasten death. They prayed their whole life to live this moment fully. If I were to give advice to my successor, I would tell him to be vigilant and to advance with prudence. Hospitals must remain places where we feel safe. Certainly, medicine saves lives. But we have to watch out for ideological abuses."

Every day, the former Father Abbot recites Saint Pope Pius X's Prayer for the Dying: "O Jesus, adoring Your last Breath, I beg You to receive mine. Not knowing at this time whether I will have command of my senses when I leave this world, I offer You even now, my last agony and all the sufferings of my death. From today on, I willingly and freely accept from Your hand whatever kind of death will please You with all its suffering, its pains, and fears. You are my Father and my Savior. I place my soul in Your hands. I desire that my last moment be united with that of Your death and that the last beat of my heart be an act of pure love for You. Amen."

Among the deaths that have impressed him, Dom Forgeot remembers that of his first Father Abbot. Father Édouard Roux died in 1962. He was sixty-six years old. Influenza was raging in the region. Several monks were bedridden. The Father Abbot had contracted the disease, but he seemed to be resisting the epidemic better than others. One night, the infirmarian noticed with concern that he had a very high fever. The village doctor did not see the tragedy coming. Dom Roux died the following day, as the Angelus was ringing on the feast of Saint Joseph. He had had time to receive Extreme Unction.

The death of Dom Jean Roy was more tragic. In 1977, at the age of fifty-six, he died suddenly from a heart attack. He was in Rome for the *Congresso* of Benedictine abbots. One morning, he collapsed in front of the door to his room. An infirmarian tried to resuscitate him, but he departed a few moments later.

The community was saddened and disoriented. To return to Fontgombault, the convoy that was transporting the body stopped at the two abbeys that he had founded, at Gricigliano, in Tuscany, and at Randol, near the Auvergne mountains. Dom Forgeot is convinced that Dom Roy felt his last hour approaching: among his things, the monks found a prayer about death that he had just copied. In

1976, the Father Abbot had wanted an architect to come prepare his tomb. The private secretary had written a letter to carry out his request, in which he indicated that nothing was urgent. In rereading the text, Dom Roy had written in the margin: "What does he know about it?" One evening, he had confided to Dom Forgeot that his days on this earth were numbered. Yet he had just had a heart exam that did not show anything in particular. Dom Forgeot has not forgotten him: "He was wonderful, courageous, honest. We owe what we are to him."

Fontgombault is fortunate to have a doctor among its monks. Since 1984, Dom Damien Thevenin has been responsible for Fontgombault's infirmary. Trained as a radiologist, he entered the monastery in December 1977, two days after defending his thesis. The young medical doctor did not live long in the world, and he regrets nothing about his former life.

Dom Thevenin is amazed to see how little modern deaths resemble those of the past: "The monks are men of their times, and they are better cared for than their predecessors. Diseases that once rapidly led to death in our time willingly take on a chronic guise. What is especially new is the refusal to look death in the face. We would like to forget it and avoid all the sufferings and anxieties that go with it."

For a monk, death must be available. It is the last act of life and the first step in the adventure of eternity. The offering can only be conscious. From this point of view, Fontgombault considers heavy and continuous sedation, as proposed by the Claeys-Leonetti Law, unacceptable and immoral. For the community, if brief sedation given to terminally ill people to help them through a difficult stage and to calm almost unbearable anxieties, like those of a patient with difficulty breathing, is legitimate, a deep and continuous sedation associated with the withholding of food and water, as the law advocates, is not: it is a form of euthanasia that the artifice of wording cannot conceal.

In 2000, an eighty-four-year-old brother had stomach cancer. After an operation to remove the cancerous tumor, he fell into a coma. The monk was on an artificial respirator, but he responded to certain requests from his brothers. He perfectly recognized his visitors. An anesthesiologist, however, decided to turn off the machine without telling Dom Thevenin. The religious died. The monks had made clear that they wanted to be present at the moment of his death. Obviously, it was a matter of getting rid of a case that was already lost and was overburdening the service. The surgeon had not been informed of the decision, either. Fontgombault expressed its anger and sadness. From that point forward, the monks have been vigilant. They pay special attention to the drafting of "advanced directives" that the hospitals offer to carry out.

Dom Thevenin has accompanied some twenty monks to their death. He has never witnessed any spectacular death agonies. The monks were serene and peaceful. One might speak of progressive stages. They let go little by little, in increments, supported by the prayer of their brothers. In a situation of dependence, the threshold for tolerance changes. The monk accepts things that seemed impossible a few weeks before.

If immediate consciousness can weaken, Dom Forgeot is convinced conversely that "the meaning of prayer remains until the final moment. Prayer is a surrender into the hands of God. How could it stop at the very moment when the encounter approaches? A patient with a brain tumor can no longer say the rosary. But the intention of the act, which consists in wanting to be with Mary, cannot change. The forms of meditation and contemplation change, the essence remains the same. The comatose monk still lives with God. The mystery of death and resurrection is at the center of his life."

Naturally, a father infirmarian gets attached to the patient. The connection can be strong. He has to know how to protect himself. Sometimes, he has to be firm, like when a sick monk refuses to take his medications: "Saint Benedict calls for caregivers with generosity and great patience. He gives the supernatural reason for this: the infirmarian must see Christ in his sick brothers and serve them accordingly. In return, the sick know they are served in honor of God. They cannot grieve the infirmarians with superficial demands. The monk in charge of caregiving is not a domestic servant. The strength of a monk's prayer throughout his life will influence his approach to old age and death", attests Dom Thevenin.

A bedridden monk often keeps his reflexes as a good religious. He looks for his rosary, he remembers prayers. Monastic formation endures. The monk dies as he has lived. He does not choose either his sickness or his suffering, but his death still resembles his life. Dom Forgeot thinks that "the stronger the supernatural life, the greater the familiarity with the afterlife, and the simpler the death. Though a criminal who repents at the very last minute will also depart in peace."

Death requires preparation. In the Litany of the Saints, we find this request: "From sudden and unexpected death, deliver us, Lord." Before the progress in medicine, death could be swift and painful. The monk had to think about and anticipate his death. "We all know that we are going to die. We should live life accordingly", concludes Dom Forgeot.

Formerly, at the time of monastic profession, the brother, prostrate on the floor, was covered with a funeral pall, symbolizing the death of the monk to the world and the beginning of a new life. Dom Guéranger had kept this practice, although he thought it theatrical. It fell into disuse when the pall proved to be too small to cover the seven Benedictines who had made their profession on the same day!

At Fontgombault, the father infirmarian is always close to the sick who are going to depart. A doctor, he easily recognizes the signs of the death agony. The irregular breathing, weakening of the pulse, and paling of the complexion do not lie. The Father Abbot is then alerted. Sometimes it is possible to assemble the whole community, sixty monks. Together, they listen to the prayer of the dying: "Go forth, Christian soul, from this world, in the name of God the almighty Father, who created you, in the name of Jesus Christ, Son of the living God, who suffered for you; ... May you live in peace this day, may your home be with God in Zion."

The infirmarian is in charge of preparing the dead body. It is a delicate moment. He undresses the deceased. The death agony can cause significant perspiration. In some cases, Dom Thevenin places the body on a stretcher for a quick shower. Then, sometimes it is necessary to shave the beard of the dead.

For the monks, the deceased have a right to the greatest charity. Dom Pateau agreed with this, elaborating that "care of the body of the dead is aimed not so much at a carnal shell as at the memory of the person. Respect for the monastic corpse shows that it is not a mere mass of cells. A soul has escaped; his flesh and bones have a right to the attentions of those who lived with the deceased.

We keep with some emotion the objects that belonged to the deceased. A watch, a habit, a notebook will become precious. The body possesses the same singularity. But it is not a matter of disguising the dead man to make him look younger or more joyful. This practice turns into a carnival and turns the deceased into a made-up mannequin. These theatrics try to reassure the living. The departed monk, laid out on his bed, is the center of attention. It calls to mind a brother whom we love. The corpse invites an encounter with the soul."

Dom Thevenin always allows an hour to pass before beginning the preparations. He believes this quiet time has a meaning. Then, the monk is clothed in the black robe with a stole on top of this if he was a priest. A man always has a past of shadow and light. But the peace that follows death is striking.

The monks accord importance to the vigil before the funeral. The gathering with the deceased is a spiritual farewell. For the father infirmarian, in particular, the departure resembles a small liberation. Death brings a kind of peace to the doctor. God reclaimed his rights. Joy is appropriate.

Dom Forgeot remembers little Brother François. He was the first civilian welcomed inside the walls of Fontgombault after the return of the monks. In October 1991, he had caught a bad case of flu. Before dinner, the Father Abbot went to give him the blessing of Compline. "Brother François, what are you doing?" The monk answered: "I am praying for our archbishop of Bourges. The novice master requested it." Archbishop Pierre Plateau was in fact hospitalized at Val-de-Grâce for an infectious disease. The doctors thought he was lost. Brother François' condition continued to decline. The ambulance arrived to take him to the hospital. He died passing through the abbey entrance at the exact hour when, for forty-three years, he had been praying on his knees before Our Lady of a Happy Death. One week later, Archbishop Plateau recovered. His doctors were never able to explain the extraordinary cause of his recovery. Two months later, filled with emotion, he came to pray at Brother François' grave to thank him.

Are old monks afraid of death? Sometimes they are attached to a life that has become soft and languid. Fear of death is related to that of the unknown. Dom Delatte thinks that they are very rare, those who want to leave the world: generally, the web of our life is totally destroyed, and we try to hold on to the last shreds. People rarely ask God to cut the final thread.

Saint Francis de Sales spoke of the "high point of the soul". The dialogue between each monk and God remains a mystery. It does not show on the outside. God allows monks to take multiple roads. One day, a Benedictine confided to Dom Pateau that he had had suicidal thoughts since the age of fourteen. He had entered a monastery where he still lives. The monk compared these moments to being enclosed in a box shut on all sides. The only possible way out was death.

A Father Abbot cannot force a soul. The psychological realm is not the spiritual realm. It is necessary to accompany the brothers who suffer and leave the intimacy of faith to God. Dom Pateau speaks of a dimension of service.

The Father Abbot of Fontgombault seeks to protect his own "from the disturbing aspects of our modern societies". He takes the example of the father cellarer's role. In an abbey, he is in charge of practical life and the material relationships with the outside world. In the Middle Ages, it was he who was responsible for supplying the store-room, for the food, and for the expenses of the community. "Today," he tells me, "this stewardship role is much more difficult. The complexity of the economy and data processing has changed everything."

It makes Dom Pateau wonder if man still has time to die. The acceleration of technological life overwhelms until the final moments. God must force us to take this time: "He says: 'That's enough', when modern man would readily answer: 'I don't have time.' We would be quite ready to miss the high point of this life. Man has become a slave. In the same way, he no longer has time for himself and for God. The lack is cruel. He does not have time to die because he does not have time to live. For his part, the monk agrees to lose all his time for God. Monastic life is happy; monastic death is, also."

Dom Pateau believes that the answer to modern egoism resides in spiritual childhood. Far from naïveté and weakness, this attitude requires a burst of strength.

The Father Abbot is struck and impressed by the simplicity of monks' deaths. He is convinced of the unity between the Fontgombault of the earth and that of heaven. No separation exists. In his *Notes sur la vie spirituelle* (Notes on the spiritual life), Dom Paul Delatte wrote: "It remains, then, that to leave the religious life of time, there is only one honorable process: to enter into the religious life of eternity, to make this solemn profession that is called death and that should be called life. Only then will we truly begin to live. This is not a paradox or just a way of thinking about things."

For the monk, after death, the essence of life continues.

The monks of Fontgombault like to speak of the acquiescence of the soul at the moment of death. It can no longer express itself in a worn-out and suffering body. A spark can no longer shine if the fire is extinguished. The journey is ended, the sick person can depart: his brothers are there.

VII

How to Say Goodbye

Mondaye Abbey

How I love being atop these mountains
That rise up to the sky,
From a gracious diadem,
Crowning this beautiful countryside.[1]

These verses from Racine, written while admiring the
Chevreuse valley, from the Château de la Madeleine, and

[1] Jean Racine, "Ode II", in *Le Paysage ou les promenades de Port-Royal-des-Champs, Oeuvres complètes*, vol. 1 (Paris: Gallimard, coll. "Bibliothèque de la Pléiade"), 1931.

the grounds of his beloved Port-Royal Abbey, could easily come to mind for the canons of Mondaye when they go on walks on the heights of the Bessin, by way of Jahouët road, which opens onto a vast landscape, up to the English Channel and the spires of the Bayeux cathedral.

Saint-Martin of Mondaye is an abbey lost in the boscage. At the edge of the little village, the Premonstratensian buildings exude balance, simplicity, and discipline.

In the heart of this deep countryside, lulled by the cock's crow, time has stopped. The town hall, near the Third Republic-style primary school, the discreet houses, the old cemetery, and the beautiful château create an enchanting bucolic setting.

The canons' church, with its cupola, towers over the area. It exemplifies the precepts of the Counter-Reformation.

Large majestic paintings, numerous statues of saints, the Blessed Sacrament chapel, all faux marble, the tombs of the abbots, made with large black or gray slabs, the woodwork and elaborate choir stalls, the diaphanous Norman light that shines through the clear stained-glass windows—this is the décor for the offices and Masses of the canons of the order of Saint Norbert.

The purity of the classical style of the architect Eustache Restout was buried under the bourgeois tastes of a devout and anxious nineteenth century. Yet this church with its outdated ornamentation is gentle and intimate. The romantic charm of this place does not define the truth of this abbey. For good influences come from the simplicity that emanates from the community.

I came to Mondaye on a Sunday evening in May. When I arrived, the brothers were finishing Vespers. The liturgy was solemn and austere.

Before dinner, I was able to admire the beautiful farm and its imposing entrance pavilion, facing the abbey. The croaking of the frogs in the large pond did not seem to bother the young religious who was praying while tending the flowers.

For three days, I observed with admiration these canons who never ceased working for God. They came and went without showing the least sign of fatigue.

The cloister, its windows, the Chapter room, decorated with large paintings by a student of Maurice Denis, the rich, opulent library, with sixty thousand volumes, create a setting where the brothers can rest from the rigors of canonical life, structured according to the rule of Saint Augustine. Because, on top of the exercises of the regular life are added those of pastoral ministry, with the parishes and chaplaincies for which the canons are responsible.

In the refectory, through the beautiful windows, I glimpsed the old cemetery of the religious who died before the return from exile. It was far from the abbey, at the edge of the park, a bit abandoned.

In front of the façade overlooking the gardens, in the middle of a vast lawn, the stone cross of the Trappistines, who briefly occupied this place during the Restoration, seemed to protect the canons.

When I returned inside the church, my eye was drawn toward a tombstone more recent than the others. A bouquet of wildflowers was placed there. Letters stood out on the stone:

HIC JACET
RR.DD.IOEL HOUQUE
QUI NOVEM PRAEFUIT ANNOS
HUIC ECCLESIAE
MMIV-MMXIII
CARUIT VIRIBUS HAUD VIRTUTIBUS
OBIIT DIE XXV MARTII A.D. MMXV
AETATIS SUAE AN. LXIX

"Here lies the most reverend Father Joël Houque, who governed this church for nine years (2004–2013). Strength failed him, courage did not. He died March 25, 2015. He was sixty-nine years old."

I knew a little about the life of Father Joël from the enthusiastic stories that Father Emmanuel-Marie from Lagrasse Abbey had told me. After his death, the canons had printed an *In memoriam* card. In the photograph that accompanied it, the forty-seventh abbot of Mondaye had a broad smile. His features were marked by disease, his laughing and melancholic eyes showed a religious whom life had not spared: "Joël Houque was born in Le Maisnil en Weppes, in Flanders, February 8, 1946. After a good education (École Supérieure de Commerce Paris), he entered Mondaye Abbey August 6, 1969. Having worked in Laos, in lieu of military service, then as a professor at the Lemonnier Institute in Caen, he made his solemn profession August 28, 1981, and was ordained a priest April 24, 1983. At the abbey, he was the bursar and master of novices (1984), sub-prior (1986), prior (1988–1999), and a priest at Saint-Paul de Vernay. He devoted himself unreservedly to the service of his brothers, while maintaining a strong pastoral concern. He loved to teach, preach, and celebrate. After having been prior of Conques (2001–2004), he was an administrator, then abbot of Mondaye (2004–2013). His time as abbot was happy and fruitful in vocations and embellishments to the monastery. After his resignation, for health reasons, he served for another year at Frigolet Abbey in Provence. Returning to Mondaye, he died March 25, 2015, on the Solemnity of the Annunciation of the Lord."

A generous man, of an anxious nature, Father Joël especially possessed the charism of the humble. He wanted to be of service to his brothers and to men. He was impatient, pragmatic, and lively. His enthusiasm, his kindness impressed his friends. Despite his influence, he did not take himself seriously. He liked to refer to himself a strange aphorism in the form of a joke: "A beautiful bird does not please everyone."

Father Joël often spoke about death. In 1990, disease had knocked at his door. During a blood donation, a doctor discovered he had slowly developing leukemia. Father Joël was realistic. He knew he would be joining God faster than his friends. When he first became abbot, he thought so much about the disease that it became his only topic of conversation. He wanted to know everything about the symptoms and treatments for his cancer. He even participated in discussion groups on the Internet.

In 2000, Father Joël began chemotherapy. He went to the Caen hospital for the day. He was tired. But the treatments allowed him to have a true remission. In 2006, he was elected Father Abbot even though his brothers knew his state of health. The gamble bordered on madness. Defying Father Joël's cancer, the canons thought he was the right man for Mondaye. At the end of his abbatial blessing, he gave this wonderful speech: "The trust that the brothers have shown me is a sign of hope that says no one can be reduced to his disease."

Father Joël was abbot for nine years.

In 2007, he began a second round of chemotherapy whose efficacy was short-lived. The disease had become more aggressive. The magnitude of his task weighed on his health. In a monastery, the abbot is the man who must lead his community. He guides the brothers. How can someone be the leader when oxygen is lacking?

In 2010, Father François-Marie Humann was named prior. His mission was to help Father Joël. Born in 1970, a graduate from an agricultural engineering school, he is the descendant of a large family, rooted in the region for centuries. Over time, the young canon become his spiritual heir. Despite the suffering, Father Joël did everything to pass on the best to Father François-Marie. He paved his way.

Little by little, the treatment caused a painful and serious pulmonary emphysema. This pathology leads to a progressive destruction of the pulmonary alveoli and blood vessels. Father Joël had to agree to receive respiratory help. At first, an oxygen station was installed in his room. Then, he decided to take a bottle of oxygen around with him, which he carried with a shoulder strap. Even in the church, he could no longer do without this machine that made the awareness of his cancer omnipresent.

The canons admired his courage. Despite the cruelty of his disease, he never complained. He continued to go up and down France to visit priories. He even managed to plan his trips around his equipment and elevators, so as not to tire himself out.

But his shortness of breath caused chronic fatigue. Periods of rest no longer allowed him to recuperate. His resignation became obvious. Father François-Marie helped him during this difficult time. Elected by the brothers, he succeeded him on October 15, 2013.

For six months, Father Joël went to Frigolet Abbey, near Tarascon. He needed to find solutions for organizing the future of this house in the south of France.

Every week, he sent letters to the canons of Mondaye. February 15, 2015, Father Joël wrote: "Dear brothers, Thursday, I went to the Avignon hospital to meet Dr. Slama, head of the hematology department, around forty years old and full of energy, who told me that new treatments are available and that, at the beginning of March, after further tests, he is considering a new chemotherapy. But it is true that the symptoms of great fatigue are now very frequent."

The last letter, dated March 8, shows a fighter who is drawing on his last ounce of strength: "Dear brothers, I spent the week in my room-office-chapel. This morning, I went down for Mass. Bishop Dufour celebrated it with a congregation of a group of travelers. Health-wise, I was rather shaken. I hope that next week will be better and that I will get a little of my breath back. Because the breath in me is terrified." This is the last sentence written by his hand for his brothers. Father Joël was not afraid of death, but he was afraid of dying badly. He knew his existence could end in a tragedy, in a brutal fit of suffocation. His lung problems turned into an obsession. Talking about it was a way to exorcise the fear.

The final week, in his big abbey, he was so tired he was becoming bedridden. Father Emmanuel-Marie came to see him. He was struck by his courage. Back at Lagrasse Abbey, he called Father François-Marie right away to alert him to the gravity of the situation. The latter convinced Father Joël to return to Mondaye to rest. He arrived Tuesday, March 17, 2015.

In Paris, where he made a stop, a brother saw him crying. Father Joël oscillated between anxiety and solace. He was happy to return, but he was afraid his trip would be the last. The canons welcomed a man who could no longer stand. However, in everyone's mind, he was coming to rest. No one wanted to believe that the end was near.

The day after his return, his condition had improved. On Thursday, March 19, the feast of Saint Joseph, he celebrated a final Mass in his room. In the afternoon, he saw his doctor. The latter did not want to hide the truth about his condition from him. Father Joël was devastated.

The next day, the respiratory attacks got worse. He was in a state of semi-consciousness. At the end of the afternoon, after hesitating, the canons decided to take him to the Bayeux hospital. From a spiritual point of view, they would have preferred that the patient be able to stay at the abbey. Hospitalization was primarily a rational choice. The suffering was becoming too intense.

The canons made the decision not to leave him alone for a moment, not knowing how long the vigil would last. Arriving at the hospital, Brother Hugues, the infirmarian of Mondaye and a doctor by training, told the emergency doctor: "Father Joël is at the end of his life. It is not a question of resisting." When he heard this remark, Father François-Marie was shocked. He could not resign himself to accepting the inevitable. He did not deny the gravity of the situation, especially since Father Joël had become practically aphasic. But the idea of his death was unacceptable to him.

The father infirmarian did not want Father Joël's death to be postponed. He knew that the price to pay of additional suffering made no sense. He wanted to avoid a tracheotomy. The doctors decided on a non-invasive ventilation that the patient did not tolerate well.

Day and night, the canons, as well as Father Joël's relatives, took turns at his bedside. The doctors and nurses were impressed by this succession. Father Joël no longer spoke. Sometimes he opened his eyes.

On Monday the 23rd, Father François-Marie was alone with him. He did not know if Father Joël heard him. But he kept telling him that he could depart. This sentence was important. Father Joël had always been a man of duty, and he was capable of resisting death so as not to abandon his brothers. Father François-Marie sensed a force that was preventing him from breaking free. That evening, he leaned over him to embrace him and say goodbye. Father Joël seized the cross around his neck and held it a long time.

The final two days, Father Joël sank into a comatose state. The former Father Abbot died on Wednesday, March 25th in the early morning. Remembering this moment, Father François-Marie told me: "He always liked to get up early and enjoy the first hours of the day. The hour of his death was consistent with his life. At the moment of his departure, we were chanting Lauds of the Annunciation."

Father Paul-Emmanuel, prior of Mondaye Abbey, a man of great sensitivity, and one of the faithful at Mondaye were with him at the moment when he departed. They were the last to keep vigil: "We were soothed by his breath, which diminished with each moment. Father Joël had always been afraid of the way he was going to die. He did not want to suffocate. In the final moments, his breathing became so weak we could no longer hear it. The shape of his face changed, his skin was increasingly pale. The expressions of his suffering disappeared. I was holding his hand to reassure him. I was praying with confidence. I talked to him until the end. The final breath was imperceptible. A beautiful life concluded in the hands of God." The prior informed the community. He was calm. He did not feel that he was living through a painful time.

A brief half hour after the death, Father François-Marie arrived: "He was beautiful. The body had been lightened to allow the soul to depart. His face was relaxed." The people who came to gather in his room had the same feeling—the impression that his body had become a spiritual reality.

Quickly, the community asked for the return of the deceased. He was placed in the Chapter room, transformed into a glowing chapel. The coffin was in the same place where Father Joël had received the habit of a canon. This large room is the antechamber of heaven. There, prostrate on the floor, the canons live the beginning and end of their religious life. There, the novice is clothed by the abbot, and the deceased, by God.

Just before the funeral, the Father Abbot François-Marie covered the face of his predecessor by lowering the hood of his cape.

The canons smilingly remember an anecdote from these lengthy days. The brother cellarer had ordered a coffin. When it arrived, the canon was surprised to discover that the interior was completely padded and decorated with lace. After a moment of reflection, the Father Abbot and Brother Arnaud took some scissors and cut out the awful, gaudy lining so as to remove anything in poor taste.

The canons were losing a father. A pillar in their lives had crumbled. Tears rolled down the faces of many faithful. The sadness did not get the better of them, but the emotion was difficult to overcome.

For the Father Abbot, it was a big responsibility. At the moment when a brother dies, he returns to God the mission that was entrusted to him. At Mondaye, the community numbers thirty canons. Father François-Marie was acutely aware of the gravity of his responsibility: "I must be humble and give everything to God. Death is difficult, unsettling. We must strip ourselves. God helps us naturally."

The liturgy of the dead was overwhelming.

According to the tradition of the canons, at the beginning of the celebration, the head of the coffin was placed against the altar, as a sign of veneration.

In his homily, with the beautiful modesty that characterizes him, Father François-Marie declared: "As an elderly brother told me, in a typically Norman understatement:

'He wasn't just anybody, Brother Joël!' That's why, even if our pain is really there, we can say a deep, big, genuine thank you. That is the meaning of this Mass that we are going to celebrate: in recommending to God the salvation of our beloved brother Joël, let us welcome the peace of God and give him thanks for the work he accomplishes in his servants. He fought for such a long time, with so much strength and courage! How could we not be deeply troubled by this sudden collapse that finally carried away our brother Joël: it is the loss of a son, a brother, a friend, a guide, a father!"

The canons are sons of Saint Augustine. Their relationship to death is marked by this heritage. Tears are easier than for other monks. The Benedictines, Cistercians, and the Carthusians do not have hearts of stone. Their feelings and their pain are as strong. But the Premonstratensians base their spiritual life on the texts of the bishop of Hippo: "I neither hoped that he would come back to life nor made my tears a plea that he should; I simply mourned and wept, for I was beset with misery and bereft of my joy. Or is it that bitter tears match the weariness we feel over what we once enjoyed, but find attractive no more?"[2]

The graves of the canons are in the communal cemetery, but the Father Abbots repose in the canons' church. Today, the memory of Father Joël is still alive, inexhaustible. He still warms hearts. Every day, the canons pray for him. Going up to the sanctuary, the brothers pass by his tomb. They think back to all the years when he was the first to arrive in the church for the offices.

[2] Saint Augustine of Hippo, *The Confessions*, trans. Maria Boulding, O.S.B. (San Francisco: Ignatius Press, 2012), 82.

Before his death, Father Joël loved very much to come pray near the funeral stone where he knew he would be buried. This location delighted him because he imagined that one day, before the beginning of Mass, the children would come running over the tombstone.

At Fontgombault, Dom Forgeot had told me that the monks died as they had lived. Father François-Marie has a slightly different opinion: he hopes "that we die better than the way in which we have lived. We must hope for this progress! The sanctification of Father Joël accelerated in the final months. He died in the odor of sanctity. At the end of his abbothood, he was radiant in himself and not because of his office. He wanted to serve. I had the feeling that there was nothing in him that had not been given."

Sometimes the canons organize walks to the cemetery after the coffee hour or in the evening before Chapter. These few steps are a little recreation. The religious often tell the same stories. They speak of the dead they have known and remember anecdotes and memories. The Premonstratensians always end by wondering where they will be buried, in which row, under which tree, next to which brother ... The walk ends in bursts of laughter.

In recent years, the parents of certain brothers have asked to be buried near them. They are not necessarily from the region, but they hold the grants in advance in order to be close to their sons.

The death of Father Vincent, in 1995, regularly comes up in the discussions. Originally from Champagne, a former member of the Free France resistance, a friend of General de Gaulle, whose daughter he had married, a cultivated and distinguished man, he was a remarkable canon. He spent the last days of his life in the Caen hospital. One morning, his doctor called the abbey to tell them his days were numbered. The Father Abbot at the time and a canon left without delay. On the way, the abbot stopped in a co-op to buy a bottle of champagne. When they arrived at the hospital, the dying man was in a bad way, but clearheaded. Turning toward the abbot, with his tone of voice a little high, he said: "Oh, my Father, you have come, it is too much of an honor!" And the abbot responded: "No, it is not too much of an honor. You are going to die. I come to give you Extreme Unction." After a moment of silence, Father Vincent responded: "Ah yes, it is necessary." Reassured by his reaction, the Father Abbot took out the good bottle from his satchel: "But afterward, we are going to celebrate!" Father Vincent let out a sigh: "Ah, you thought of it . . ." The three canons celebrated with the champagne. Father Vincent died in peace two days later at the abbey.

A full community is composed of the living and the dead. The canons' present is nourished by the memory of the dead. When the canons are in the choir stalls, which date back to 1743, they know that many brothers have gone before them. They do not necessarily know their names. But they do not forget them.

In general, the young brothers who enter Mondaye have never had contact with death. The departure of an elderly brother is always a discovery. They grow familiar with death. They learn to say goodbye.

We forget men of power. Father Joël was not one. But it is difficult to recover from the death of a servant.

Today, a father is missed by his brothers.

Before leaving Mondaye, on a beautiful sunny morning, I returned to the famous tomb. The wildflowers had disappeared. An anonymous hand had left white lilies there.

VIII

The Deaths of the Recluses

The Grande Chartreuse Monastery

In the austere library of Fontgombault, my attention was drawn to an old book in which biographies of saints were collected. I spent a long while reading an entry about Bruno.

A few lines about the founder of the Grande Chartreuse are enough to draw the reader into mysterious lands. Admiration and curiosity rise like waves during a spring tide:

Saint Bruno. Day of death: October 6, 1101. Tomb: in the monastery of Saint-Stephen, at La Torre, in Calabria. Life:

Saint Bruno is the founder of the Carthusian order. Along with Saint Norbert, he is the only German founder of an order. He was born in Cologne, around the year 1030; his contemporaries call him the light of the Church, the flower of the clergy, the glory of Germany and France. The persecutions by Manasses, the simonist archbishop of Reims, made his resolution to retire into solitude develop and mature (1076). After a brief stay at Molesmes Abbey, where he spoke with Abbot Robert, the bishop of Grenoble, Hugh, assigned him as his residence a place that took its name of "Chartreuse" from the surrounding mountains. The order founded by Saint Bruno is one of the strictest that exists in the Church: the Carthusians adopted the rule of Saint Benedict, but added to it the obligation of silence and abstinence from all meat (they eat only bread, vegetables, and water). Saint Bruno wanted to revive the ancient hermit life. This order is renowned for having never been unfaithful to the spirit of its founder, so that it never needed to be reformed. Six years after the founding of his order, Bruno was called to Rome by Pope Urban II to be his advisor. He went only reluctantly. But, when the pope was obliged to flee from Emperor Henri IV to Campania, Saint Bruno discovered a deserted place, similar to Chartreuse, where he founded a second residence that became a flourishing monastery. It is there that he was struck, in September 1101, by a serious illness. He summoned his disciples and made before them, in the manner of an apostolic profession of faith, a public confession; after which he died, at the age of seventy-one.

The Grande Chartreuse is the result of a mystical encounter between a place and an ascetic, a great alchemy, the transfiguration of a landscape by the silence of hermits. Dom Dysmas de Lassus, minister general of the order, repeats that he tries to fight against the myth that surrounds his monastery. It would take him several lifetimes to succeed ...

On that beautiful day in July 2017, it was nine-thirty in the evening at the Grande Chartreuse. A pale, red light flooded the horizon, striking the walls, the forests, and the crests of the mountains. The narrow valley was already sleeping, and I was the only one to stay up to contemplate the sunset falling over the monastic city.

On summer evenings, when the hikers leave the trails and the monks close their shutters, silence envelops the still nature. There are only the owls to let out long, magnificent hoots. Far off, the barking of sheep dogs is sometimes heard.

The little houses of the sons of Saint Bruno are surrounded by high mountains that completely encircle the whole countryside. High above, flying over the Charmant Som, a plane passed through the sky. I imagined life in the cabin. Below, in their humble cells, the Carthusians were piously asleep. During the day, the monks who walk in their little gardens see the planes passing above them. What do they think then? Are they secretly praying for passengers going to unknown destinations?

Two hours later, the sky was sprinkled with stars and the bells were joyously ringing. The monks were opening their eyes; they had finished the first part of their night. After the solitary recitation of Matins de *Beata*, they went through the long corridors of the cloister to attend night office.

I crossed the vast gallery of maps to reach the gallery in the church. It was twelve-ten A.M. I saw the brothers enter the sanctuary plunged in complete darkness. The Carthusians slowly reached their stalls. With help from small torches, they prepared the liturgical books in which they could follow the psalms, the responses, the antiphons, and the hymns. Night prayer is long, between two and three hours. That day, we returned to our cells around two-thirty in the morning.

Matins began, and the church remained in darkness. The chanting of the psalms, solemn, profound, had never seemed so beautiful to me. The Carthusians know them from memory. The red flame of the Blessed Sacrament was the only light. Then an angelic voice, as pure as water from a spring, began the reading from a text of Saint Irenaeus.

These moments of grace are the heart of Carthusian life. Every night, the Carthusians offer this wonderful prayer to God. Lauds followed Matins; the austerity, the starkness, the beauty of these chants stunned me. There is nothing comparable to the Carthusian offices.

Leaving, I saw a postulant wrapped in a large black cape, the hood raised over his head. He was walking unhurriedly back to his cell. Every night, until his death, he would come to sing the great night prayer.

The door that opened onto the corridor of officers was open. I heard the wind picking up. The courtyard of honor was still and deserted. The delicate lapping of water in the stone basins resounded gently. At the Grande Chartreuse, singing is never accompanied by instruments. There is no organ. The only music comes from the works of nature.

The next day, I stayed a long time in the cloister. The doors of the thirty-two pavilions remained closed. Generations of monks have walked on these old stones. But the silence has never varied.

To go to Mass, Vespers, the night office, the fathers pass through these galleries. According to custom, they leave their cells without a word and walk as closely as possible to the walls.

During the summer, the windows of the cloister are open to the interior courtyards and the cemetery. The light colors walls already patinated by the centuries. The Carthusians try to retain a bit of warmth. Then they can better see the graves at their doors. Sometimes birds come in, like curious little visitors.

In the winter, the wooden crosses marking the location of graves bend and yield under the weight of snow. Night falls quickly, the wind carries the echoes of the tall pine forests, and the murmuring of the snow speaks instead of the monks.

This summer morning, an elderly brother was walking slowly in the endless corridors of the Grande Chartreuse. Filled with emotion, I watched him advancing with measured steps with the help of a wooden cane. In work clothes, his back injured, he carried a large wicker basket. Despite his ninety-three years, Brother Michel-Marie was in charge of sewing. He stopped in front of the cell doors to collect the clothes that the fathers needed mended.

The old lay brothers never stop working. These worker brothers are awaiting God, but they do not like to leave the last word to time, which passes. They want to continue the work as in the early stages of their lives.

In 2015, one of them, Brother Joachim, had to go to the hospital. The Carthusians remember that he had no longer wanted to eat the day he understood that his faltering health would prevent him from going back to work. The brother was the bursar; in the language of a Carthusian, this means that he took care of organizing the meals alongside the brother cook.

In general, the brothers who can no longer work devote themselves entirely to saying the rosary. Brother Marie-Bernard remained thus for years in his cell, between two stays at the hospital to fix his legs. He was simply waiting, as if this situation were the most natural in the world. Several years before his death, he decided that Saint Joseph would come to get him. And in fact, during Lent, he had declined. But March 19 had arrived, and Saint Joseph did not come. Brother Marie-Bernard was a little disappointed. For three years, he had watched for the feast of Saint Joseph without anything happening. In the end, he was right. The monk died on March 19. At the moment of his death, the end-of-winter sun was dazzling.

Brother Louis had become completely deaf. He had worked all his life on the vast roofs of the Grande Chartreuse. Overtaken by the unproductiveness of old age, he prayed continuously in his cell. During the night, he came to the church. Despite his deafness, he followed every office in the big books. Around two o'clock in the morning, the old Carthusian died returning to his cell. Without a sound.

Brother Hilaire died at the age of ninety-nine. For as long as he could, he participated in the liturgy, remaining at the back of the brothers' choir. Dom Innocent told me about him: "I remember his last week, in the cell where we had kept vigil over him for several days. It's a distant memory, but I still see his oratory completely lined in pious images, so much so that you could no longer see the wood. He died without complications. One day, we were told he was dead, and that was all."

The deaths of the fathers of the cloister are often even more extraordinary. From a human perspective, they are almost incomprehensible.

The death agony of Dom Landuin made an impact on the Carthusians. This monk, born in 1925, was gifted with a tenacious character and a resilient spirit. During recreation, Dom Landuin spoke little. He was tough, laconic, humble. One day in Lent 2015, after Vespers, he wanted to speak with Dom Innocent. They left for the Chapter room. Quietly, Dom Landuin told him: "I am tired. I am going to die the day after tomorrow or maybe Sunday." The monk tried to reassure him. Dom Landuin continued: "In any case, I am certain that it will be before the end of the year." He had spoken these words calmly. The prospect of his end made him serene. He was sure that God was approaching him. And, indeed, Dom Landuin died within the two months that followed his little prophecy.

He had begun to arrange his things for his successor. In his role as archivist, he had accumulated an incredible mass of papers and books that were strewn on the floor of his cell. Two weeks before his death, he was obliged to give up night office. Dom Dysmas suggested he move to the infirmary so he could be closer to the church. He always declined this offer.

Dom Landuin continued to burn the documents he judged useless, and the Carthusians came to give him Communion in his room. His fatigue became evident; Dom Dysmas wanted to call the community's doctor. Dom Landuin's response was final: "What would you want him to do? We must leave this earth." Already, he was hardly eating anymore.

One Sunday evening, Dom Innocent asked him if he would agree to being watched. Carthusians live lives of solitude. They dream of preserving this eremitical existence until death. However, Dom Landuin was not opposed to the monks coming to pray in his room. They came to visit him in turns.

He was not suffering. He was gently slipping toward God. The Carthusians were witnesses to this slow walk of their brother toward eternity. The second night of the vigil, Dom Landuin stopped speaking. The old man had become a little aphasic child. One morning, his breathing stopped for long seconds. But the body was holding on.

The day of his death, the Carthusians present around his bed all had the same feeling: the Virgin Mary and the celestial court had descended to come take him by the hand. In this little gray room with walls covered with soot from an outdated wood-burning stove, the floor still strewn with loose papers scribbled by his hand, a son of Saint Bruno left the world. Dom Landuin was radiant.

For the hermits, the indigence of the place, the emaciated face of their brother, the poverty of care were not important. They saw only the light that radiated from his face. Dom Landuin died without suffering during the great night office. Discreetly informed by Dom Foulques-Marie, the prior left the church to go to his cell.

The monks understood that their brother had just died. In their stalls, they continued the prayer. Dom Landuin had entered the Grande Chartreuse in 1950. He had flown away without a word.

In the middle of the night, helped by two other Carthusians, Dom Dysmas prepared the body. They put his white habit back on him and the rosary of his profession. Then they placed him on a plank in the center of the room, and Dom Dysmas lit the Paschal candle, a symbol of the Resurrection.

The death of Dom Landuin left a particular imprint. It deviated from the customs of the recluses. There really is a Carthusian way. A beginning full of enthusiasm, a middle of difficult and contrasted experiences, then a peace that announces eternity. When the Carthusians arrive at the end of their road, they are already detached from life.

Brother Jean was found dead in the oratory of his cell. One evening in 2010, he died with his eyes fixed on the ivory crucifix that had supported his prayer for half a century. The Carthusians found him the next morning, on his knees, his hands joined and eyes closed.

Dom Gabriel had breathing problems. Up until the last day of his life, he wanted to go to the church. He walked the long halls with a bottle of oxygen. He died during Mass. After Communion, seated in his stall, Dom Gabriel lowered his head. He never raised it again.

Dom André Poisson was the minister general of the order and prior of the Grande Chartreuse from 1967 to 1997. In 2005, he died alone during night office. He was afflicted with Alzheimer's disease and cancer. But he never suffered. The Carthusians had not seen his end coming. Dom André died two days before the general Chapter: the priors of all the monasteries around the world were at Chartreuse. So, they were all present for his funeral. This sign touched the monks.

A few months before his death, some novices went to greet him. Brother Marie-Pierre asked him how long he had been at Chartreuse. Dom André answered: "It is sixty years." He was silent for a moment before adding: "Sixty years, it goes by quickly!"

Dom André was a very honest man. A graduate from the École Polytechnique, a former resistance worker, he had chosen to renounce a promising career to enter the Grande Chartreuse. In a sermon given on the occasion of the nine-hundredth anniversary of Bruno's arrival in the valley, he had described the character of the founder of the order. This portrait was a bit his own:

And yet, Bruno was not a sentimental person who allowed himself to be guided by superficial impressions. Others have already noted how important the notion of utility was to him. Not, certainly, in the sense of a human achievement to be conquered, but in the sense of a life that must bear authentic divine fruits. Bruno was a practical man. For him, contemplative life did not consist in entertaining streams of sublime thought: it was a matter of using effective ways of reaching God. He was perfectly aware that his solitude was the place where "he opened himself to very busy idleness and perfectly relaxed activity. Here," he said, "for the price of effort in battle, God gives his fighters the awaited recompense: the peace that the world does not know and joy in the Holy Spirit." In the same way, from the moment when the grace of conversion pierced his soul, he did not procrastinate. Concrete decisions immediately followed: to leave the world, to take the monastic habit, to seek eternal realities. The choice was made: he bound himself by a vow.

On Sundays, as a general rule, Dom Jacques attended to the spiritual meeting of lay brothers. He left the recreation of the fathers a half hour before it finished. That day, he got up, and, contrary to habit, he said: "This is it, it is time, I am leaving you." Ten minutes later, he died alone on a staircase leading to the cloister.

At the Grande Chartreuse, there is no death agony. It is rare that sick monks suffer. They die serenely, in the perfect solitude of their cells. "Dying alone is part of our charism. This death resembles us", Dom Innocent sums up with humor.

Some Carthusians at the end of life are no longer able to eat. They die, then, like fledglings fallen to the ground. In the final weeks, Dom Marc, who was blind, took only one glass of milk a day. One day, his heart stopped. The community did not have time to keep vigil with him.

The Carthusians are not afraid of leaving this world. The cemetery is in the middle of the large cloister. Every day, beginning in the novitiate, the fathers have walked beside the enclosure in order to get to the church.

When a Carthusian dies, the whole community gathers in the cell of the deceased for the lifting of the body. The body is led in procession to the church. In the choir, between the stalls, the deceased is no longer alone. Near the body laid on the floor, the monks pray for him.

The Carthusians themselves dig the graves that welcome the bodies of their own. The deceased is secured to a simple board lowered into the clay soil. The cemetery is not large; regularly, the monks have to empty the old graves by hand to make room. The skulls and bones are first set aside before being put back in the grave at the same time as the new body.

Traditionally, the latest novice to enter the monastery holds the processional cross, placed at the foot of the grave. It is he who most clearly sees the body of his elder and the hood lowered over the face.

According to the directives of Guigues, fifth prior of the Grande Chartreuse and legislator of the order, who wrote the "Statutes of the Carthusians" at the beginning of the twelfth century, the head of the deceased is turned toward the conventual church. The young monk watches the four Carthusians designated by the prior to throw in the shovelfuls of dirt, sometimes pebbles, to close the grave. He hears the muffled sound of clumps of earth that fall on the body. The verb "to bury" takes on its full meaning. The community waits until the grave is filled.

Dom Innocent told me with his usual humor that life would be a disaster if we did not know that death would come for us one day. How could men remain indefinitely in this valley of tears? "We are born to meet God. The old Carthusians ask him not to delay. Death is the end of school. Afterward comes Paradise. A monk has given his life to God, and he has never met him. It is normal for him to be impatient to see him. As in the poems of Teresa

of Avila and John of the Cross, the Carthusians die from
not dying. To our great regret, the Holy Spirit is not in
a hurry to come for us. In our order, purifications and
great trials are not common. In the final months, Christ
has already taken hold of our elderly monks. The worn-
out body returns to the earth, but it is to await the glory of
its resurrection. We do not know yet what our body really
is, its beauty, its glory, and its light. The most beautiful, by
far, is yet to come."

In speaking with the Carthusians, I realized there were not
many who died of cancer. Two or three monks had had a
tumor; but they were spared suffering. The brothers think
that the rigor of the Carthusian diet explains their good
health. The Carthusians, including the sick, do not eat meat.
The fathers do not eat breakfast. For half the year, from
September 14 to Easter, the great monastic fast, they dine
on a simple piece of bread with fruit juice or a glass water.
The only meal is lunch. In Carthusian language, they call it
a pittance. It consists of eggs or fish and vegetables from the
kitchen garden. During Advent and the fast that precedes
Easter, the Carthusians abstain from dairy products.

Since the founding of the order, funeral days have been
considered moments of celebration. The Carthusians eat,
as an exception, in the refectory; in ordinary times, they
come here on Sundays and for solemnities. If the funerals
fall on a fast day, it will not be observed. In the evening,
they will also have a full meal in their cell.

After the burial, the community meets in the Chapter
room. The prior gives a sermon and recalls the life of the deceased. In general, during the recreation that follows the
funeral, the Carthusians speak of the brother who just died.

They can come into the chapel of the dead to reflect
near the bones of the first Carthusians from the eleventh

and twelfth centuries. A few paces from the cells, the companions of Bruno sleep in this sad and somber oratory. Their ancient skulls rest under the high altar. On hiking days, the Carthusians come to this place to pray before leaving to climb the mountain trails.

In the cemetery, there are no names on the graves. On one side, thin, black wooden crosses indicate the graves of the fathers and lay brothers. On the other side, stone crosses are reserved for the last earthly dwelling of the priors. The Carthusians choose to disappear from the eyes of the world and then from their own brothers. Often, they are incapable of finding the precise grave of a monk in the cemetery. The hermits die without leaving a trace. Forgetfulness immediately follows death. The dreadful phrase from Genesis comes to mind (3:19): "In the sweat of your face you shall eat bread till you return to the ground, for out of it you were taken; you are dust, and to dust you shall return."

At the end of the enclosure, however, two small, discreet graves bear the names of the dead. One day, on the occasion of the annual family visit, the father of a monk died from a heart attack during his sleep. He was staying in the beautiful building of the exterior guesthouse. The family asked that he be buried in the cemetery of the monks. The Carthusians agreed. He rests beside the father of Dom André Poisson. The night that preceded the solemn profession of his son, death came for him, too. The young Carthusian thought it was a confirmation of the action that was going to see a page of his life turned. These two men are the exceptions in the cemetery of the Grande Chartreuse.

Saint Bruno himself left few traces. He sent only two letters that allow us to grasp his spirituality and thought. The Carthusians themselves know almost nothing about his life. In a homily from 1983, Dom André Poisson could say: "It is thus a kind of stylized image of our Blessed Father that Providence has wanted to present to our love and our devotion."

In the same way, monks who write books simply sign them "A Carthusian". Men often make great efforts to leave a trace. In all the Carthusian monasteries of the world, the attitude is the opposite.

Unlike the oldest monastic traditions, the Carthusians are reluctant to write biographical notes about their dead. Some brothers request that their death not be announced. Even in eternity, they are afraid of being recognized.

The desire for obscurity is so strong that few Carthusians have been canonized. The priors have never spoken of the lives of their most exemplary monks. Dom Innocent sums up the situation with a saying that does not lack spirit: "The Carthusian monastery makes saints; it does not publish them."

In the nineteenth century, the monks made an astonishing discovery. While digging a grave, next to the oldest ones, they came upon a perfectly preserved corpse. Its preservation, after decades in the ground, was a miracle. The monks ran to the Reverend Father. His response was final: "Close the grave, dig next to it, and don't tell anyone about it." Similarly, in the middle of the seventeenth century, in the cemetery of the old Carthusian monastery in Paris, at the site of the current Luxembourg garden, miracles were multiplying on the grave of a lay brother who had died in the odor of sanctity. Dom Innocent says the prior came to the place to address the deceased: "In the name of holy obedience, I forbid you to perform miracles." The extraordinary phenomena ceased immediately.

The Carthusians who have had important duties in the order are nonetheless worried about the future of the work they have done. So it was for Dom Maurice, who was the novice master for thirty-five years at the Carthusian monastery of Sélignac, then at the Grand Chartreuse. Generations of young monks were impacted by his demanding and rough instruction. Before his death, Dom Maurice wanted to know who would succeed him. In 1990, Dom Dysmas came to tell him of his nomination to the position he had occupied. Dom Dysmas corresponded in every way to the choice for which he had secretly hoped. A few short weeks later, he left this world reassured.

The solitary life of the Carthusians is often the source of great human and spiritual richness. Their ways of dying are radiant with this freedom.

Solitude is also a field of combat. Paradoxically, resistance to God is stronger outside the world. In a homily for the feast of the Ascension, 1984, Dom André Poisson described, in a few perfectly chosen words, the truth about the eremitical existence: "Our life in the desert is beautiful; it is attractive. But it lays bare the fragilities of our heart insofar as it tests the legitimate attractions of our nature."

The beauty of Carthusian deaths, sweet and simple, seems to bear witness to the fact that the spiritual combat of the sons of Bruno is so powerful that, in the final hour, fears are abolished. In the last moments, the peace that dwells in them is so profound that the majority of them are not afraid to die alone. They have spent their lives in the silence of an austere cell that sees them leave this earth.

For these men, death is a final exam that is easy to pass, and eternal life is like summer vacation. Earthly life is a simple school for understanding God. Students are not made to sit on benches facing a blackboard. After the exam, they leave on other paths.

Saint Teresa of Avila compared life to a night in a bad inn. Dom Innocent imagines existence like a night on a train: "The important thing is not the journey but the place of arrival. I spend half my life thinking about eternal life. It is the constant backdrop that lines my whole existence. I am not afraid of the Grim Reaper. It makes me curious. Eternity passes through death. We must love this door that will allow us to know the Father. We are born for heaven. Earthly life and eternal life are intimately connected. Why fear the junction between these realities? Christians no longer really believe in the resurrection of bodies. Paradise is likened to a void of floating souls. But men are in the image of God. It will not be necessary to leave our humanity in order to be united with God. Eternity will be much more human than we can imagine. We should cultivate an imaginary image of eternal life."

The Carthusians often feel the limits of this world more strongly than men plunged in the thick of everyday life. They have a keen sense of the incompleteness of earthly life.

Dom Innocent knows by heart the beautiful poem by Charles Péguy, from *The Portal of the Mystery of Hope:*

The faith that I love the best, says God, is hope.

Faith doesn't surprise me.
It's not surprising.
I am so resplendent in my creation....

Charity, says God, that doesn't surprise me.
It's not surprising.
These poor creatures are so miserable that unless
   they had a heart of stone, how could they not
   have love for each other....

What surprises me, says God, is hope.
And I can't get over it....
Hope is a little girl, nothing at all.
Who came into the world on Christmas day just
    this past year....
This little girl, nothing at all.
She alone, carrying the others, who will cross
    worlds past....

Faith is obvious....

Unfortunately Charity is obvious....

But hope is not obvious. Hope does not come on
    its own.
To hope, my child, you would have to be quite
    fortunate, to have obtained, received a great
    grace....

Faith sees what is....

Charity loves what is....

Hope sees what has not yet been and what will be.
She loves what has not yet been and what will
    be....
On the *uphill path, sandy and troublesome.*
On the uphill road.
Dragged along, hanging from the arms of her two
    older sisters,
Who hold her by the hand,
The little hope.
Pushes on.
And in between her two older sisters she seems to
    let herself be carried.
Like a child who lacks the energy to walk.
And is dragged along the road in spite of herself.
But in reality it is she who moves the other two.
And who carries them,
And who moves the whole world.

And who carries it.
Because no one ever works except for children.

And the two older ones don't walk except for the
youngest.[1]

Little Hope is the salt of Carthusian life. The Carthusians
have left the whirlwind of the earth. Yet, they still have a
keen awareness of the fragility of human ways. They know
that the actions of this world bear weight in eternity. The
inspiration of these men is in the Apocalypse of Saint John
(Rev 14:13): "And I heard a voice from heaven saying,
'Write this: Blessed are the dead who from now on die in
the Lord.' 'Blessed indeed,' says the Spirit, 'that they may
rest from their labors, for their deeds follow them!'"

The hope of the Carthusians is so great, they place so
much confidence in God, that they often receive their
doctor with a cheerful detachment. For example, one day,
an elderly monk, near death, met with the monastery doctor. The doctor said: "How are you?" The answer was not
very precise: "Much better than I deserve." And the doctor retorted: "That doesn't tell a doctor anything!"

The Carthusians remember a number of equally surprising anecdotes. Dom Guigues was having disturbing pains.
The doctor came urgently. After a few moments, he told
him: "This is serious. You could die!" And the religious
replied without stopping to think: "Well if it's only that ..."

Dom Robert also consulted a doctor. The latter questioned him: "How are you?" His response was some-
what equivocal: "Me, I'm quite well. It's my health that's
rather bad."

[1] Charles Péguy, *The Portal of the Mystery of Hope*, trans. David Louis Schin-
dler, Jr. (Grand Rapids, Mich.: Eerdmans, 1996), 3–12.

Dom Ferdinand Vidal, Dom André Poisson's predecessor, greeting a nurse, answered in his own way: "Reverend Father, how is your health?" Dom Ferdinand explained that everything was perfectly fine. Then he listed fifteen infirmities that were attacking him and that would have led any other man to the emergency room.

For a Carthusian, illness is as simple as death. Does a hermit want to die? Dom Innocent responds simply: "God decides. Modern society presents death in an unappealing way. We must move away from this vision. We must accept the darkness of the earth and wait impatiently for heaven."

A few weeks after my trip, Dom Innocent sent me a note: "You had asked me if I were waiting for death. I did not say yes right away, for a basically obvious reason: it is not the door I am waiting for, but what is on the other side of the door. I am not waiting for death, but for Life. This should go without saying, but curiously enough it is not so common. Perhaps I reacted this way because I often take a little walk, in faith and in imagination—what I call 'dreaming'. But when one knows that the reality is even more incredible than the dream ... then, yes, there is a little impatience."

In a Carthusian monastery, in the eyes of the world, nothing happens. The existence is monotonous. After death, lost in an anonymous cemetery and without history, the memory of the sons of Bruno vanishes. A Carthusian, who wished to remain anonymous, confided to me in a solemn voice: "Your book will be a rare exception. For the first time, we will speak of our lives and of our deaths."

The hermit monk does not turn back to the past. He is on his way to God. In this land of slowness and humility, the stones of the Grande Chartreuse are the only ones to remember the monks.

The beautiful cloister of the officers looks like a wonderful road. Near the monumental gate, a stained-glass window represents Saint Bruno. The head bent down, he protects his sons, and the thousand-year-old motto of the order: "Stat crux dum volvitur orbis" (Above the changing world, the cross remains immutable).

The day of my departure, I was able to enter the cell of Dom Landuin. Two years after his death, this place remains unchanged. The blackened walls, the straw on the plank of the cupboard-bed, a few papers, a few books, some blank leaves of paper, the old rough floor, the little window looking onto the abandoned garden: a view of the poor surroundings of a solitary life was presented to me. Outside, the sun was shining. The birds were singing, and a few buzzing insects entered through the workshop window. The simplicity was dizzying.

Then, while packing my suitcase, I saw far off a young lay brother who was hoeing in the garden of the reverend father. The man was taking care of the community vegetables. He was sparing no effort. Sometimes, he raised his head, caught his breath, and then continued his humble labor. The vegetable garden is just a few hundred yards from the cemetery. Not far from God.

EPILOGUE

A Bus in the Night

When he was the master of novices, Dom Dysmas once took a postulant to the six A.M. bus. During the night, the two men went down to the little main road, near La Correrie.

In the winter, from the Grande Chartreuse onward, it was necessary to make your way through thick snow. Often, gusts of wind slowed the walk.

Below, the bus stop was not marked. An edge of the road, nothing more. Dom Dysmas and the postulant waited patiently. Headlights in the distance. The bus? No, just a car. The time had not come yet. When it finally appeared, Dom Dysmas immediately recognized its illuminated strip. They had just enough time to give each other a hug, hail the driver, load the suitcase. Farewell. One minute later, the bus disappeared into the darkness of the forest, out of sight, and Dom Dysmas remained alone on the side of the road.

For the monks, death is not so different.

In telling me this story, Dom Dysmas spoke softly, with eyes full of kindness: "It's an old friend who drives the bus; we wave to her as she passes, indicating that, the next time, perhaps it is you whom she will take for the beautiful trip. Or someone else, who knows? But we must leave that to God."

THOSE FOR WHOM THE
ROAD BEGINS

Brother Vincent, Father Michel-Marie, Dom Landuin were links in a great chain. They have walked the paths that generations of monks have taken before them. They have also seen the new generation of religious who would bring them to the cemetery. These men knew they were not alone.

During my travels, I spoke with the young monks, the successors of the brothers to whom I have dedicated this book.

At Lagrasse, I remember Brother Jean-Marie, a prodigious musician, who illuminated the ceremonies with his music. Often, I could hear him at the organ, alone in the church, or at the piano. The notes escaped into the majestic courtyard of honor.

At Solesmes, in the refectory, the long table of novices was in the middle. The youngest of the sons of Saint Benedict listened attentively to the reading of the day. From the pulpit, Dom Geoffroy Kemlin enunciated each syllable with precision and made an age-old text wonderful.

At the Grande Chartreuse, a Dutch student in his twenties had come to spend ten days to reflect on his vocation. That afternoon in July, I can still see him, in jeans and sneakers, a bit lost, in the gallery of the church where it is possible to follow the offices. During night prayer, another, more seasoned aspirant had helped him to follow along in the Latin antiphonaries. A few months later, I learned that their visit had borne fruit. They were considering entering the Carthusians.

At Sept-Fons, vocations were abundant. Dozens of young Trappists were sitting in the stalls of the sanctuary. Joy and cheerfulness were visible on all the faces. After Brother Théophane, they were spring buds in the garden of God.

The graves of the pious monks whose lives and deaths I have had the honor of recounting will not be covered in weeds. The novices will come to pray for their masters in the faith.

The cemeteries of the abbeys will always be in bloom.

Sept-Fons, April 17, 2017—Paris, January 1, 2018